Hi Lonette,
Hope you enjoy this
Book. Stephany is a
longtime friend.
Janet
7/2012

UNTOLD STORIES OF A

Real Estate Diva

STEPHANY SOFOS

DEDICATION

To my father and mother, Tom and Rena,

My greatest mentors who continue to inspire me everyday,

And for Nalu, the best friend I could ever have.

ACKNOWLEDGEMENTS

This book could not have been written without the continuing encouragement of my friends, Frank Mento, Marilyn McPoland, Valerie Sylvester, Janet Fox, Renee Osborne, Jen Heider, Bill Redeker, and Barbara Del Piano.

Frank is my muse and the person who started me on this writing journey. Were it not for him, these stories would never have been told.

Marilyn, Valerie, and Renee, for the past several years, have always cheered me on and they are the ones off whom I have bounced most of my storylines, seeking their input and insight.

Thank you, Renee, for being my cover girl and for your friend Jonathan Higa for his excellent photography.

Janet Fox is my adopted, or *hanai,* Mom who babysat me when I was a little girl and has been as close to me as my own mother.

I am grateful to Jen Heider of Whizzbang Studios for the graphics on the cover of the book.

Bill Redeker has given me feedback and written the foreword for this book, for which I feel honored.

Barbara Del Piano, one of my greatest mentors, is a published author in her own right. She volunteered her time for editing this work. I could not have completed this endeavor without her.

Many thanks to each of you for your never-ending help and encouragement.

FOREWORD

With its blue skies, sunny beaches, and swaying palms, Hawaii has rightfully earned the nickname, "Paradise."

But in *Untold Stories of A Real Estate Diva*, long time real estate broker and appraiser Stephany Sofos takes readers behind the scenes of "postcard Hawaii" into a real life world of deceit, corruption, sex, and even murder. Like Monte Carlo, Hawaii can sometimes be "a sunny place for shady characters."

As a correspondent for both ABC and CBS networks, I frequently covered Hawaii for many years. I got to know Stephany at her favorite haunt, the Outrigger Canoe Club. She was an invaluable source for understanding the various booms and busts in the real estate market. She also had a keen understanding of island history, socio-economic conflicts and local politics.

Stephany has literally been inside thousands of homes from the most meager island shacks to the most ostentatious beachfront estates. That access and the people she's met along the way have made her uniquely qualified to reveal the truth behind the state's sun splashed veneer.

From selling residential real estate, to managing shopping malls, to working with developers, Stephany thrived on hard work. She was also considered outspoken and too aggressive by some, which resulted in her being fired more than once. Eventually she ended up working for herself and became known as one of the top real estate brokers and appraisers in Hawaii. That gave her instant credibility with news reporters who would frequently call for interviews.

Along the way, *Untold Stories of a Real Estate Diva* reveals the back room deals, sexual trysts and scandals that form the backdrop of a fascinating career. As a result, there are lots of lessons learned.

This is a book about discovery for both the author and the reader. It's also a tale about the evolution of modern Hawaii. From the break up of feudal land ownership, to the Donn the Beachcomber era, to the scandals of Ron Rewald, to the explosion of McMansions along Hawaii's breathtaking beaches. No wonder so many of the characters in this Tell-All have had their names changed to mask their identities. Stephany has taken the reader on a journey behind the scenes of this place everyone calls "Paradise."

Bill Redeker

Bill Redeker is a former television news correspondent who reported for ABC and CBS News for more than three decades. A six time Emmy Award winner, he has also won Peabody and George Polk Awards, as well as an Alfred I. du-Pont Columbia University Award and Overseas Press Club Award for Foreign Affairs and Investigative Reporting.

PREFACE

All the stories in my book are based on true situations and events. In some cases, the time and location has been altered. Certain names have been changed and physical characteristics have been altered to protect the identity of those mentioned and are noted by an asterisk. Other names have been used with permission. Well-known personalities appear as mentioned when applicable.

Stephany Sofos
June 2012

TABLE OF CONTENTS

CHAPTER ONE

The Reluctant Realtor

Life is so interesting. It never goes as you imagined no matter how hard you try. Take me, for instance. I never really wanted to be in real estate.

My Dad and Mom were immigrants from Greece and came to Hawaii during World War II via the United States Navy. They got into the business in the late 1940s' with their company, TASCO Realty, Inc. With Dad as salesman and general contractor, and Mom as accountant and payroll master, they built over two-hundred-fifty homes in Waialae-Kahala. They went on to build houses on the ridges of East Honolulu and apartment buildings in Waikiki, Kaneohe, and Kalihi.

However, the business of home building was then, as it is today, feast or famine, and it was no different for Mom and Dad. Often, they, as the developer/contractor, would have just enough money until the next house was sold and there were times we had to move out of our home to a smaller place when there wasn't enough money to pay the bills.

I can still remember the day my mother came to see the nuns at St. Andrew's Priory where I went to school, and ask for a deferment of tuition because as she told them, in front of me, there wasn't enough money for groceries. They understood and smiled at me as we drove away in her brand new 1963 shiny, black, convertible Cadillac to our about-to-be foreclosed brick home in Kahala. They recovered in the latter part of the year, but as I learned at an early age, insecurity is a staple of the profession.

I also thought, from my observations growing up, that the sales side of the real estate profession was mainly for retired military guys who desperately wanted to get out of the house and escape from their wives (and go down to the neighborhood bar and drink themselves silly to forget their war experiences). Or for spoiled doctors' and attorneys' wives who needed to be "working" because lunching every day at the private clubs got so boring for them.

I imagined being a professional surfer with sun-bleached hair and a toned, tanned body escaping to exotic locales with hot surfer dudes and listening to the Beach Boys and Ricky Nelson. I had experienced my own Ryder Smith as in "Where the Boys Are." And we really did have our versions of "Beach Blanket Bingo." Life for many of us was truly about sun, surf, sea, and a little tennis.

In the waning days of the Vietnam War, Hawaii was in transition from the primary "R & R" (Rest and Recreation) center for servicemen coming back from "The Conflict," to a glamorous resort experience for the average American traveler. Many of the older local folks still held on to the "plantation days" philosophy with its subtle racism, and many were fearful of "the domino effect" coming true, with our state being so close to that troubled continent of Asia. The younger people were clueless in their provincial thinking, stoned most of the time, hating the War, and the military in general.

Pidgin English was the dialect of choice to distinguish locals from mainland "*haoles*" (Caucasians) or foreign-born Asians. There was instant rapport with other locals, just by nodding and saying, "Howzit, Brah?" or "How you Auntie?"

I was an okay college student at the University of Hawaii at Manoa, but was more interested in being outdoors…surfing and playing tennis than studying. Sports were more important to me than history and economics, but I made it through in four years.

Unfortunately for me, I was a good surfer, but not a great one. My good friend Evie Black, who became the United States surfing champion, was both an inspiration and a nemesis. She and Traci Phillips, a three time kayak Olympian, often surfed where I did and would eat my ego for lunch with their moves and fearlessness on the big waves.

By the time I graduated from college, I didn't know what to do. Working part time stringing tennis racquets and selling the latest fashions to the next Jimmy Connors and Chris Evert at "The Tennis Ball" in Kahala Mall was not going to compensate for the $500 monthly room and board my father insisted I start paying the day after my college graduation.

My brother, Steven, who majored in real estate at UH, and who immensely enjoyed the wheeling and dealing of the commercial sales side of the business said, "Come work with me at Aaron M. Chaney, Inc. Real Estate is in our blood, it'll be fun."

I had already acquired my real estate salesman's license the previous year as I thought it would help me to understand marketing and statistics. So I thought to myself, how hard can it be, selling houses, selling tennis balls, same thing, just a different package and product.

Twenty-one years old with no money or marketable skills, looming debt to my father, and my brother's encouragement, I started on my new career as a residential real estate sales agent.

As I was leaving with my brother on my first day of work, Mom was sitting at the dining room table in her white silk Japanese kimono reading the morning paper. She looked up and could see the anxiety on my face. She smiled, had a sip of coffee, and gently said,

"Stephany, don't be 'The Reluctant Realtor'. I know you will be fine."

I thought to myself, God I hope so because I'm sweating in all these clothes and makeup and my damn nylons itch.

CHAPTER TWO

My Name Is Danielle, Not Danni! *

Working in Honolulu in the 1970s was anything but glamorous for women. In those days, very few ladies held positions of power in business and only a very small number had college degrees. Most women were secretaries, bookkeepers or assistants.

However, there was one woman of substance, and every woman working in downtown Honolulu recognized her when they saw her around town. That woman was Madelyn Payne Dunham, President Barack Obama's grandmother. She was someone to remember because she was so rare and had "made it" as an Assistant Vice President of Bank of Hawaii.

It seemed Mrs. Dunham was outside the small convenience store at the Financial Plaza of the Pacific when I came by for coffee every morning. She always wore a suit with a flowing bouffant tie, which was popular in those days. Her hair was always in a bun; she wore glasses, dark red lipstick, and never smiled. With a cigarette in one hand, and a cup of coffee in the other, she was usually engaged in a heated discussion with a co-worker about some situation going on at the bank. She was small in statue, but large in toughness. You could discern her no nonsense attitude from ten feet away, and you could see she was stronger then nails. Mrs. Dunham had to be tough back then, because discrimination was strong and women were not thought of as equals or assets, but more like chattel.

After about three months of seeing me everyday, she finally grunted a "hello" in my direction and I was thrilled, as she was a hero to so many of the lowly women of Honolulu, especially me. Over the next couple of years, while I worked at Aaron M. Chaney, Inc. we actually got to the "Good Morning" and "Have a Good Weekend" stage, but she was always so involved with her job, I understood that there was no room for dialogue with anyone beyond her own sphere of work.

On the first day of my new career I thought I had dressed well; I wore a little makeup, black skirt, white blouse, nylons, and close-toed shoes. I had worn mostly shorts, tee shirts and rubber slippers during my four years at the University, and prior to that, seven years of uniforms at St. Andrew's Priory.

However, compared to the other real estate women in the office, dressed in power suits, designer dresses, the men in suits and ties; there was no question...I was not a match. My fashion sense was nonexistent to say the least, and if anything, very conservative. Fashion is still pretty much a non-issue for me as I find it all a bit frivolous and still gravitate to dress shorts and polo shirts.

Our workday began at 9:30 a.m. sharp when we were marched into the conference room to take our seats. The seating was by financial status, not seniority; the greater your income production, the closer you sat to the front of the table where coffee, doughnuts and sales material were located.

At 9:35 a.m. on the dot, in walked this woman, 5' 11", 220+ pounds, dark pinstriped pants suit, short, cropped, black hair, black glasses, and thick silver jewelry on her neck, wrists, and fingers, as was the style back then.

Her hands were enormous…strong, rough, dark, like farmer's hands, which is exactly what they had been back in her home state of Tennessee. She looked around the room at the twenty-two agents present (fifteen men, seven women) of which there were twelve of us "newbies" and said, "My name is Danielle, not Danni." She waited a moment, then continued, "If you call me Danni, even once, you and I will have a problem for the rest of your days here. I am your sales manager and everything goes through me. You will not do anything without my permission. You will not send out letters, write offers, or go to Brokers' Opens without my knowledge and approval. You will sign in and out when you leave the office so I will know where you are at all times."

She then went on to discuss the company's current listings, projects, escrows, and policies. As she ended her presentation, she made her final announcements and continued, "Lastly, let me make this perfectly clear to each and everyone of you. We are in this business to make money, plain and simple. Only hard work is what will make you wealthy, not college degrees."

With that comment, she turned, took off her glasses, and glared straight into my eyes as everyone turned to look at me. I turned beet- red and lowered my eyes, thinking to myself, oh God, I am so screwed!

CHAPTER THREE

"Sex In The City" - Residential

Like a storyline in HBO's "Sex in the City," when a house or apartment is listed for sale, the agency gets a set of keys for the property. The keys go into a Lock Box, and in order to see the property, the agent, has to sign out for them. To pick up keys from the offices of other agents, you must show your photo identification and return the keys within a few hours. But back in the 1970s through the 1990s, you were frequently allowed to keep the keys for a 24-hour period. Within the first month of starting my new profession I learned about "The Club".

The Club was a group of agents around town who would check out properties and deem which ones were good for having sex and parties and then discreetly let each other know where and when to go for a bit of clandestine fun.

Typically, these properties were vacant and furnished, had good privacy, no nosey neighbors, and most importantly, a washer and dryer to clean up afterwards. The trash was always disposed of so it wasn't sitting for days in the apartment or outside a presumably empty house. Some properties were also the model units of new condominium developments which agents frequently showed after hours so the "client" could see and fully appreciate the evening "views" from the location.

When a good place was found, word got around to members of The Club, and everyone was very careful not to arouse the suspicion of the sales managers. It was understood that no one would go to the same property more then three times in two months, as listings usually took three to four months to sell back then.

One of my associates, Robert Maccie*, was a master of the Club, until his wife Gloria* caught him several years later. However, during the years I knew him, he was a great player. He was a well-known realtor in the community and had lived all his life in Kailua. In his middle 30s, tall, 6' 3", dark, handsome, and thickly athletic with emerald green eyes, Robert found the best places in town for his "horizontal hula," as he facetiously described it.

"Rule Number One, never play in your own backyard," he always warned anyone willing to listen, and which for him meant never going to Kailua. He and his main playmate, Nicki,* who was also married and a real estate agent at a different company, visited these places once or twice a month.

After their "hula," other agents were often invited over to party, drink wine, eat pupus, and enjoy a beautiful sunset in a well appointed home while listening to soft music as the washer/dryer finished its last cycle.

In today's world, there are Multiple Listing Service messages that say, "Listor Must be Present to Show" to avoid such "situations". Electronic key systems have also evolved which alert the listing agent of someone's entry and exit to the property, and record identifications, with the amount of time in and on the site. And with "Nanny Cams," and close proximity to neighbors who are home all the time, the Club has greatly diminished.

However, more often then not, some agents, when given an opportunity where there is little chance of being caught, are still daring and adventurous. Even now I hear of agents "previewing" properties on their own and enjoying the fringe benefits of working in residential real estate.

And Robert? How did his wife find him out and what happened to him? From the story I heard, Gloria called the office one afternoon looking for him to exchange cars. A new agent at the firm, who was on the "cold call desk," and had yet to learn the dos and don'ts of giving out information, answered her call from the general line and told her Robert was meeting a client at a new listing on Diamond Head. Gloria asked for the address and he gladly provided it.

As she drove up the hill to the house, she found only one car there...his car. People familiar with the tale said she thought this odd, as the new agent told her he was supposed to be meeting the client at the property.

Assuming the client had left, she went into the house to find Robert. She knew from all her years of living with a real estate agent to go around the back of the house, and as expected, the back patio door was open to catch the cool breeze. Unfortunately for Robert, a frozen wind came in instead.

Gloria heard loud moaning coming from the master bedroom upstairs. She took off her shoes and quietly walked barefooted up the stairs and found him in the waterbed completely naked, doing the "horizontal hula" with his "client."

The story goes that she was so mad she pulled out a hair pin from the back of her head and stabbed it into the bed several times, all the while screaming at the top of her lungs. With the weight of Robert and his paramour on the bed, water spurted out everywhere and the bed exploded with the two naked lovers falling out and on to the new cherry wood floor. The water flowed out of the bedroom and down the hardwood staircase, also new, like a spectacular Nuuanu water-fall after a heavy Pali rain. Robert's afternoon tryst ended up costing him his wife, his job, and thousands of dollars for a new waterbed, bedroom and staircase flooring. You would have thought this epi-sode was his demise and that he would be ruined, but the last time I saw him, which was a couple of years ago, he was on wife number three and selling expensive German cars. He was making very good money, happy, and still as charming and handsome as the first day I met him.

Always the quintessential salesman, he hugged me goodbye as we parted and said, "Selling is selling, Sweetheart."

CHAPTER FOUR

The Business Of Real Estate

I was never really a materialistic person growing up; sun, surf, and tennis were my passions. To me, life was about being outdoors and as long as I had a good surfboard, a tightly strung tennis racquet, and friends to surf and play tennis with, I was the happiest of campers.

Don't get me wrong, I loved nice things, and still do, but for me it was always about the quality of the experience and not the quantity of possessions.

However, once you decide to get into the real estate game, it does become about material things…particularly cars, clothes, and the flow of money. At first it doesn't cost much to get into the game; real estate school and a license are the only requirements, but as you get established, it takes a lot of dollars to be a full time professional.

Advertising, networking parties, professional organizations' dues, continuing education, errors and omissions insurance, clothing, travel, lunches and dinners with clients, transportation for your clients and you, gifts for clients and vendors, etc. are just some of the expenses you find yourself straddled with, and as your business grows, your overhead increases exponentially.

I realized after my first week as an independent contractor that it took a lot of time and dollars to "play" in the sport of real estate. In the 1970s an average full time agent's annual commissions in Hawaii were around $6,000; in today's world it's about $45,000 per year. Hawaii agents have always done a little better then the rest of the United States as the National Association of Realtors stated in 2010 the national average for an agent was $34,100 per year; after 16 years in the business, earnings went to $47,100.

With my father's requirement of $500 per month for room and board, and car expenses of $100 bucks a month, it was already costing me 20% more then the average agent made to just live day-to-day. I immediately realized I had to do at least fifty percent better than the standard just to break even. How was I ever going to make that much money?

My first thoughts in those early days were that I could get a blonde wig, fishnet stockings, stiletto heels, a red dress, call myself "Veronica", and hang out on the corner of Lewers Street and Kuhio Avenue like the other type of "independent contractors" did in Waikiki. Back then I had a good figure, no boyfriend, and I wasn't doing anything much on weekends.

However, those thoughts were fleeting and the truth was, I never really mastered walking in heels and wigs itched. I understood I would need to work real estate and have a second job to pay bills until I could make enough as a full time agent. I would keep my

"Tennis Ball" gig and work my butt off to sell, sell, and sell the beautiful properties of Honolulu.

It was the first lesson I learned in real estate. The business was then, as it is now, an industry of survival. In order to be a "player" you have to spend a lot of time being in the fray of things so at least you can eat on the pieces left behind by the big guns. Kind of like what a Remora or small pilot fish does with sharks.

CHAPTER FIVE

My First Sale

One of the first things they teach you in real estate is to "farm" certain areas. "Farming" is selecting specific condominiums and sections of town and work them exclusively. This way you don't wear yourself ragged trying to know everything and can focus on particular properties and neighborhoods more effectively.

Farming utilizes various ploys to market yourself in the hope of getting people to take you on as their agent. The number one method is "cold calling," which is calling people in your chosen area, trying to solicit them as clients. "Remember fifteen nos equal one yes," Danielle always told me. Cold calling was always difficult for me and I never enjoyed it as I have thin eardrums and all the yelling and screaming from people telling me not to call again hurt my ears and devastated my self-esteem.

Other techniques of farming are direct letter writing to owners, sending flowers and small gifts to resident managers because they usually get a free apartment and small salary and are always hungry for more. These items are also known as "carrots" or "enticements" and hopefully will get your name in the buildings' newsletters and community boards. Pens, coffee mugs, calendars, and key chains with your name plastered on them are typical gifts given to owners or friends of friends of owners. Postcards showing the number of sales and listings you have are also effective in letting everyone know how successful you are.

My brother, Steven, was in the commercial and I was in the residential division of Chaney and we were immediately compared to each other and dubbed the "Donny and Marie" of the real estate world by our fellow agents. The pressure was growing daily on me to be a successful sales agent. He already had two years in the business and had learned to use postcards with recipes as one of his farming schemes. "People will keep the recipe card and remember to call when they're ready to sell or buy," he told me. I thought this was a brilliant idea and knew it wasn't original with him, not because he isn't smart, but because he can't cook for beans.

I sent out two hundred postcards each month using my mother's original Greek recipes, as I can't cook either, and Mama's food was out of this world. The concoctions were for lamb chops, salads, prime rib, stuffed grape leaves, spanakopita, and baklava.

Finally, after four months, I got a call from an elderly couple that desperately needed to sell their condominium. Mr. Louis Johnson* had throat cancer and wanted to get Martha,* his wife of 62 years, taken care of before he died. They were childless and he needed her to be financially secure.

Louis had been music director and organist for forty years at a tiny Catholic church just outside of Kona, and Martha was the secretary. They had been childhood sweethearts, meeting in third grade, and he said, for him it was love at first sight. But for her, it took until he kissed her at their Junior Prom before she knew she was going to marry him. They lived in a small farming community in Ohio, kind of like the town in the movie, "It's a Wonderful Life," and moved to the Big Island of Hawaii soon after they married.

The Johnsons' came to Honolulu after retiring a year earlier. By then his cancer was diagnosed as terminal. They both were tall, thin, and fragile, with thick white hair, fair complexions, and the brightest blue eyes I'd ever seen next to my mother's peepers.

Their apartment was painted pale yellow with a yellow and brown shag carpet, which was the style then. The place was immaculate, with pictures and mementoes of their life together. Their wedding picture hung above his electric organ, a bit faded, but you could still see their radiant smiles on that day so long ago.

The sofa and matching chairs faced the balcony that overlooked the ocean from the twentieth floor, and the panoramic views of the shoreline and Honolulu Harbor were stunning. Passenger ships, tugs, and barges, glistened in the morning sun. As I sat down, I noticed the aroma of chocolate emanating from the kitchen. Mrs. Johnson then appeared bringing hot tea with milk and homemade chocolate chip cookies. Mr. Johnson sat at his organ and asked me what my favorite classical music piece was, then played *Pacobells' Canon D*. He was a wonderful musician, even with disease and age plaguing him. They were welcoming, warm, and very trusting of me…the scared, untried, and inexperienced real estate agent.

After tea and conversation about Hawaii, Ohio, family, and health, he said simply, "We know you will help us. We believe in you."

That was it! They signed the listing agreement for the sales price Danielle had determined and I left. They were satisfied; there was no need for further discussion.

There are times in your life when you are inspired, and in those moments you become unwaveringly determined. Many spiritual leaders have stated that when you are on the right path of life, everything flows smoothly, and that was how I felt with the Johnsons.

As I walked down the hall to the elevator, I resolved to make their goals my goals, and for the first time in my fledging career, I felt empowered because I so wanted to help them.

I worked tirelessly on the telephone, made those hated cold calls, wrote letters, advertised, and sat every open house. Within 45 days of signing the listing contract I had a full-price cash offer with a closing in 30 days or less.

When he saw the offer, Mr. Johnson's eyes welled up and he said to me, "Now Martha will be safe". He died four days after the closing.

The funeral was held at Our Lady of Peace Cathedral, where St. Damien of Molokai had been ordained as a Catholic priest. The opulence of the church was amazing, combined with the smells and colors of flowers sent by their many friends in Kona. The High Mass seemed more appropriate for a Prince of the Church than a humble organist from the Big Island, but to those present, whose hearts he had touched, it was a fitting tribute.

Martha got up and spoke and said that for the last thirty days of his life, her husband had smiled all the time. She looked at me and said I was the one who put that smile on his face. She said he had wanted to give me a gift for helping them, but did not live to present it to me. So now she was going to deliver it to me.

She turned and nodded and the Cathedral's great organ with its three-story tall copper pipes began to play *Pacobell's Canon D*.

This time, it was I who cried.

CHAPTER SIX

The Language Of Real Estate

The real estate business is attractive to a lot of people as it's a good way for someone just starting out to be entrepreneurial. It's also easier to get into than most other professions because all it takes is a brokerage house to sign you on after you pass the test and receive your sales license. No college degree or apprenticeship is required.

Many people play it as a game, where the stakes are high because of the money to be made. Many people who get into the real estate business do so primarily to be independent, and hope to make a good living.

However, to make money and remain competitive, it does take long hours, certain skills, and knowledge of a "language," so to speak, which is learned over time.

One of the greatest talents is to become skilled in this terminology, which on the surface says one thing to the average person, but when translated into real estate dialect means something entirely different. It provides immediate information to those "in the know" and helps to move properties quickly.

Here are some of the key words and terms with their "real" translations:

1. "Cozy" – Cramped, tiny house or condominium.
2. "Quaint" – Old.
3. "Quaint Home" – Older house and bring your toothbrush only because there is no storage space for anything else.
4. "Charming" – House sits on a tiny plot of land and does not need much maintenance.
5. "Cute Little Bungalow" – Smaller than a postage stamp.
6. "Cottage" – A little larger than a bungalow, but still a postage stamp.
7. "Perfect for Newlyweds" – Tiny, tiny, tiny place, but who cares. Newlyweds don't because they are spending all their time in bed.
8. "Needs a little TLC" – A dump and needs a lot of work.
9. "A Fixer-Upper" – A tear down, or if it's a condominium, in need of a complete gut job.
10. "Handyman's Special" – Previous owner did everything himself and now the property needs to be brought up to building codes before a fire starts, it can be insured, and anyone can live in it.
11. "Tear Down" – Tear down.
12. "Architecturally Inspired Home" – Developer's tract house.

13. "On a Main Thoroughfare" – Traffic is merciless and children and small animals will be road kill if you let them out on their own.

14. "On a Quiet Cul-de-Sac" - Only the immediate crazy neighbors are around you, and not the mainstream nutcases.

15. "Backs up to a city park" - Good security system and a big dog will be needed to protect you from the homeless and riffraff coming onto your property claiming it's part of their inheritance because of their native hunting and gathering rights.

16. "Unique Property" - Run now! It's a dog!

17. "Recently Renovated" - Painted and carpeted.

18. "Beautifully Renovated" - Sellers themselves painted and carpeted.

19. "Totally Renovated" - Owners actually renovated the property with new kitchen, bathrooms, electrical work, plumbing, floors, paint, landscaping, and roof.

20. "Principals Only" - Sellers are too cheap to pay a real estate commission and think they know everything about real estate. Really, just ask them.

21. "Cash Only" - Owners don't want to wait for lenders because they want to get out of town quickly. Usually they are foreign nationals, and for the most part, sell among themselves.

22. "It's Not About the Money" - It's ALL about the money.

23. "It's Not About the Commission" - It's ALL about the commission.

24. "Will Take Paper" - Sales price way too high so seller will take. a second mortgage at a higher interest rate to obtain his astronomical price.

25. "For Sale By Owner" - Same as "principals only," except these owners don't really know anything about real estate and will

tell you this much; they just don't want to pay a real estate commission to those "greedy bastards".

26. "Below Appraised Value" - Sellers have the old appraisal report which was done when they purchased the property, and now that they are upside-down and values have diminished, they are peddling the property at a price close to what they purchased it for, hoping someone will be lured into the sales price with the old report showing past value and take the albatross off their hands.

27. "Motivated Seller" - Help! The property owner is sinking under the mortgage and needs a quick sale to stop the oncoming foreclosure.

28. "Willing to Look at All Reasonable Offers" - Help! The seller just got served with foreclosure papers.

29. "Not a Short Sale" - Help! The sellers are stuck in a neighborhood of houses being foreclosed and want out before they become collateral damage.

30. "Motivated Buyer" - Divorce settlement is final and he/she needs to buy something quickly before all the relatives come knocking on the door looking for "a small loan".

31. "Buyer's Remorse" - Oh God, what the heck was I thinking? It's all his/her fault!

32. "Attorney" - Deal killer.

33. "Full Service Real Estate Agent" - Someone who has not made a sale in over a year and is now doing rentals for clients because he/she is desperate for income. Also could be someone who needs cash flow because their husband or wife is trying to become a "developer" or an "artist" and hasn't contributed to the mortgage payments in a while.

34. "Cold Call Desk" - Every new agent who doesn't know much about anything rotates on and off this desk to answer incoming calls (which helps keep the costs down because a real secretary costs money). More often than not, it's an opportunity to pick up leads from people searching for an agent.

35. "Commissionectomy" - When you first bring a deal to a seller or buyer, you are loved until the transaction looks like it will actually happen. Then all of a sudden, no one remembers what you've done and everyone wants to cut your commission down because all you are is just a "sales person." This tactic is more often attempted in commercial as opposed to residential transactions. The surgeons in these procedures are almost always attorneys or large real estate companies with attorneys on retainer.

36. "Potted Plant" - Real estate agent after an agreement has been reached between buyer and seller. The agent who does all the work, but never gets the credit, which somehow ends up going to attorneys.

37. "Caveat Emptor" - Let the buyer beware, or in simple terms, be afraid; be very afraid.

38. "Cloud on the Title" - Uh oh! The sellers forgot to have the relatives from the Kentucky mountains sign off first before selling.

39. "Location, Location, Location" - The better the location, the higher the sales price the sellers will try to squeeze out of you.

40. "Peak-a-boo Ocean Views" - If you stand on a chair and lean to the extreme left, you can see a bit of ocean between the buildings in front of you.

41. "Distant Ocean Views" - Put your glasses on and focus on the horizon; after a few minutes you should see something that looks like the ocean.

42. "Garden View" - No view.

43. "Direct Ocean View" - Oceanfront, and it should be for what the sellers are extracting in sales prices.

44. "Maid's Quarters" - Illegal rental unit.

45. "In Laws' Residence" - Illegal rental unit.

46. "Sub-Prime Mortgage Brokers" - Scumbags. Former used car salesmen or real estate agents who know nothing about nothing, but dress well, and are very charming. Many prey on immigrants and less-educated people who trust them. Their clients sign mortgages and after years of paying accelerated rates, find they have no chance of holding on to their American dream of home ownership.

47. "Good Cash Flow" - If you put 40% or more down, you may break even or have a few bucks to spare for the ever-increasing real property taxes.

48. "Cash Cow" - Property that produces a large cash income without much effort. It almost runs by itself to the point that all the owner has to do is collect rent, travel, or play polo. Very unusual for Hawaiian real estate because of its high costs.

49. "Good Capitalization Rate" - The lower the risk, the lower the rate; the higher the risk, the higher the rate. In reality, this means the sellers want every cent they can squeeze out of the investment for fear the next guy who buys it will benefit from their work.

50. "Dead Fish Walking" - Bellied up or dead deal.

51. "Bird Dogs" - Also known as "runners" or "grunts." These are new agents who work for senior agents and their job is to find

new listings, cold call, or check out new projects. For all their work, they don't get much of the commission, but it's their chance to learn from the pros.

52. "Bottom Fisher" - Cheapskate. Someone looking for the lowest price and who will wait for the bottom to drop out of the market before jumping into it. Problem is, no one ever knows when it's hit bottom, and many times they get screwed because they took too long to take the plunge.

53. "Booting the Offer" - Money, jewels, personal property or your first-born child, whichever is given to make a difference in value between exchanged properties. Not used too often nowadays as the first-born is a depreciating asset with the cost of college tuition.

54. "It's a Very Ambitious Project" - Run! Run like Hell. Now! Before they ask you for investment money or you become a tenant in the property.

55. "Certificate of Insurance" - An insurance company verifies that a policy insuring certain parties, usually the landlord, is in effect, or translated, "Its the tenant's problem now, not mine! Yippee!"

56. "Code of Ethics" - A written system of ethical standards and conduct. It is often used to keep the buyer's and seller's agents' tongues in check so as not to bad mouth each other, and to show who the top dog is during the transaction.

CHAPTER SEVEN

Men Rule And Women Drool

Not long after my fourth sale, I felt good about my selling and marketing skills, but after all the expenses were paid, I was still broke and my "tennis ball" second job was ending. Bills were looming and Dad was relentless about his monthly rent payment. So I decided to ask the owner of the company, Mr. Chaney, for a "real" job with a salary.

Aaron M. Chaney was in his early sixties and an extremely proud man. He was fairly tall, trim, and a two-pack-a-day smoker. He was part Hawaiian and his family had struggled to send him to the elite Punahou School. Although he was an excellent student, he had not been able to afford college. He once told me that not obtaining a degree was something of a disappointment to him.

However, the lack of a college degree did not stop him and he did become one of the first Certified Property Managers (CPM) in the nation through the Institute of Real Estate Management of the National Association of Realtors. With hard work, a backbreaking schedule, and his wife doing the accounting, they started the company twenty-five years earlier in the disappearing days of plantation life when only Caucasian men of missionary heritage or mainlanders with Ivy League college degrees ran all businesses in Hawaii. With his six-days-a-week, twelve hours a day work ethic, he built the largest property management company for both residential and commercial properties in the state by the time I came along. He was someone both my brother and I greatly admired and he was one of the main reasons I chose to obtain my CPM designation.

Mr. Chaney always dressed in crisp, starched white shirts, tie, wool slacks, and highly polished shoes. He was very "old school" in his manners and temperament and extremely formal with most people, especially women. When a woman came into his office, he always kept the door open so no one could make any assumptions of impropriety.

The gentleman was all business and his personal office reflected this persona. It was spotless, and there was no clutter anywhere. There were no magazines, newspapers, or papers on his desk except for the one sheet he was currently working on. There were two chairs, a small couch, and a credenza with his telephone and separate photographs of his wife, son, and late daughter on it.

When I entered his office we exchanged pleasantries and he quickly came to the point. "Congratulations on your most recent sale, Stephany. What can I do for you?"

"Mr. C., I would like to become a property manager for residential properties. I have a good education, two years experience selling real estate, a designation from the National Association of Realtors, and my broker's license." Mr. Chaney listened, then leaned back in his chair and took a deep drag on his cigarette. He looked directly at me and simply said, "No". "May I ask why? Gilbert* just graduated from college two weeks ago, and has no experience or license and he got a property manager's job last week."

"Gilbert is a man and he comes with certain assets I appreciate, and as much as I recognize your skills, I just can't believe a woman has the ability to run more then one or two properties. I need a person who can manage at least five. Also, meetings are at night, and women have families and need to be home for them. I am also concerned about a woman's safety, walking to her car at night can be dangerous." He went on to say, "We do have Jennifer* who was an administrative assistant for several years and is now an assistant property manager. She is doing quite well. We could put you in an admin position and in two or three years reevaluate you for an assistant property manager.

"Mr. Chaney, I don't want to be a secretary. I can't survive on that pay, I would rather work as a cashier at Foodland. They make $800 per month, same as property managers," I said.

He stood up, indicating the discussion was over, and as he walked me out the door, he said, "That's the best I can offer, so good luck with Foodland, and if I were you, I would learn to live within my means."

After the meeting, I felt very dejected and sat down with Rebecca Hart,* another agent in the residential department. She was my best friend at the company. Rebecca was in her early forties, slightly matronly, but tall, blond hair, blue eyes and the most engaging smile. She had been a corporate business secretary and married the love of her life. Unfortunately, she told me, they were not very good at marriage and she left the relationship with her three kids in tow and moved to Kauai where she harvested *puka* shells on the beach.

Rebecca returned to the island of Oahu when she realized her kids needed a better education and a more stable life. She always dreamed of selling oceanfront properties to movie stars. She was meticulous, fun loving, level headed, trustworthy, and the best friend anyone could ever ask for. "I can't believe he wouldn't at least give me a chance when he gave Gilbert a position without any experience. I have a college degree, a broker's license, and almost two years of experience selling real estate, for God sakes," I complained.

"College degrees mean nothing here. Men rule and women drool in this company. Don't ever forget that. And of course he gave Gilbert the job," Rebecca knowingly replied. "Why, is he some kind of genius?" I asked innocently. "I don't know about that, I heard he did very well in school," she said with a sly grin, "but most importantly, Gilbert is a close relative of Mr. Chaney."

CHAPTER EIGHT

A New Beginning

I wanted out. After my meeting with Mr. Chaney I was disillusioned with the whole state of affairs and tired of Danielle's ruthless hounding. She never stopped criticizing and complaining of our team's performance because she made a good bonus on her income from our work.

I began to send out resumes to all the companies that had property management divisions. I wanted to get into property management because I had already put almost two years into the real estate business and I thought managing properties would give me a chance to make a decent salary.

I went to ten interviews in the first two months, and although some were brief and others lengthy, they always asked me the same questions:

"Do you type?"

"Yes."

"How many words a minute?"

"Sixty."

"So you are looking for a management position. What are your skills?"

"I'm a college graduate, a graduate of the Realtors Institute, and a licensed real estate broker. I'm looking for a company that I can grow with and establish my skills as a real estate professional," I answered each time.

What I really wanted to say, but knew it would kill my chances was, "Look, I'm broke, almost 23 years old, can sell tennis balls, sneakers, and real estate. What more do you want? Just give me a chance, you idiot, to show you what I can do. What's the problem? Can't you see through those glasses?"

I hoped for a job with either Bank of Hawaii or First Hawaiian Bank because of their attractive employee benefits. One morning, while waiting in First Hawaiian's colorless Human Resources Department where everything was a shade of beige, I sat beside the wife of an Army veteran. After eleven years of service, including three tours of duty in Vietnam and Cambodia, he had been honorably discharged when the Vietnam War ended.

She was foreign born Japanese and looking for a clerical position. They had two children and, she explained, all his years of infantry duty did not interest employers as Vietnam vets were not popular in those days, and his service record was no help in finding a job. She was now to be the support of the family while he stayed home with the children. She started crying while telling me her story, and I kept thinking how she needed a job so much more than I. I felt a bit embarrassed to want a job when she so desperately needed one. We exchanged telephone numbers and, I later found out, she didn't get the job. Human Resources didn't like her accent and told her so.

When I walked into the cubical for my meeting, the interviewer was a middle aged, rotund, balding man with thick horned-rimmed glasses, dressed in a polyester aloha shirt and slacks, both of which were one size too small. He appeared to be bored with his job and the people he met. As he looked me over from top to bottom, he told me that the skirt and blouse I was wearing were unacceptable attire and bank policy and dress code for women was either suits or dresses but absolutely no pants suits. These were the days when Johnny Bellinger, as Chairman of First Hawaiian Bank, ruled and he was very old school. Women were tolerated as employees, but not welcome in management.

I didn't care too much about the dress code, but was more concerned with the starting salary. I worried that the pay of $700 per month, which is what he kept indicating I would receive if I were hired as an asset manager, was not enough to pay my bills.

"Excuse me, Mr. Smith,"* I interjected, "but why would I only receive $700 per month when your ad says there is a $700 to $1,250 per month salary range. I have all the qualifications the ad calls for, plus I have experience in sales. I believe I should make more then the minimum starting salary."

I could tell he was extremely annoyed with my question, but surprisingly, he answered me. "The higher pay is for mainland people coming into Hawaii. They have certain expectations of wages. Most local folks live with family and aren't interested in leaving Hawaii. We have found what they make per month is not as important to them. A secure job with good benefits and good hours so they can be with their family is what they want and they are willing to take less to have this payback."

I was dumbfounded as I sat there listening to him and thought, "What a crock of poop! A prejudicial wage and salary policy against locals because we all wanted to live and stay in our homeland." I figured he wouldn't understand my father's demand for $500 per month for room and board, and that sometimes local people have the same expectations as mainlanders do in order to survive in Hawaii.

It turned out that I shouldn't have worried. I was dismissed after the first interview. I later learned, when I telephoned Mr. Smith, that he thought I had a bit of an attitude, was too chatty, and needed to learn my place. As he droned on about learning from the beginning and to reapply for a bank teller position with starting pay of $500 per month, I thought, "There go my hopes of a banking career."

The months went by and finally, when I had lost almost all hope, I received a called from Hawaii Management Company, a division of Blackfield Corporation, a real estate development company owned by Pacific Lighting Corporation of California.

Alan Beall, the president of Blackfield, was quite the "boy genius" in real estate development in his time. In my opinion, he was one of the most creative developers Hawaii has ever had. He had worked for various development companies during his years in the business, and Blackfield was one of the last companies he headed before going on his own. He was a progressive thinker, and his attitude, which he instilled in his management team was, "I don't care who or what you are, but what do you bring to the table?" In the 1970s, his attitude created an exciting workplace.

After three interviews I was hired as a property supervisor to manage commercial properties with a starting salary of $850 per month. Needless to say, I was elated.

Three days later, I walked into Mr. Chaney's office and asked him to sign off on my license because I had found a job in property management. As I walked out of his office, I had a big smile on my face. This was going to be a new beginning.

CHAPTER NINE

The Youngest Shopping Center Manager In America

Discovery Bay was the newest luxury condominium project in Waikiki. It was forty stories tall and directly across the street from the Ilikai Hotel which became world famous as a result of appearing in the opening scenes of the "Hawaii 5-0" television series. Built in 1976, the Discovery Bay complex was unique because it had a mixture of residential and retail condominiums. I was hired as the shopping center manager, in charge of all businesses located on the ground and second floors. The center was a large commercial condominium consisting of twelve retail shops and restaurants, with McDonald's and a grocery outlet as anchor tenants.

The McDonald's restaurant, which cost $1.2 million, was the most expensive McDonald's ever built at that time. It was my understanding that Ray Kroc, the founder of McDonald's, had a great love for Hawaii and owned a home on Kahala Avenue, which he often visited. He wanted this restaurant to express the true essence of Hawaii. The interior was built with priceless logs of Koa, Hawaii's beautiful endemic wood. The trims were copper and brass, and the décor told the ancient stories of the Islands. It was one of the most beautiful restaurants I had ever seen, and it was fast food!

I was so excited and pretty proud of myself until my new boss, Henry Neillson,* President of Hawaii Management Company, took me to the center and showed me my office.

It was a storage closet under the fire escape, kind of like Harry Potter's original bedroom, but dirtier and smellier. The janitor's supplies…toilet paper, paper towels, cleaning materials and chemicals, were stored on the floor which was covered with indoor-outdoor carpeting. There was a telephone on a small desk with a plastic desk chair like the ones you buy at Home Depot for outdoor patios. There were no windows or ventilation, and it was very hot. Henry gave me a set of keys, a manual for the sump pumps (what the hell were sump pumps?) and told me to "manage the property." Then he handed me the Yellow Pages and told me to hire temporary help when I needed it. As he left, he said he would be checking on me in a couple of days.

Hawaii Management Company had just taken over three new commercial properties the week before I started, and Henry was going crazy trying to get everyone in place. Even though he would talk with me a couple of times a day, it would be a few weeks before he had time to stop by again and have a cup of coffee and chat with me about management policies and procedures.

I was clueless and had no idea what I was supposed to do. I assumed, with no training, that I was to baby-sit the property. I could do that…make sure the trash cans were emptied and the floors and bathrooms cleaned, and that the parking attendant wasn't stealing.

The problem was, I had no employees to clean. As I stood by the telephone, looking through the Yellow Pages Henry had given me, the sweat started dripping down my nose and I took off my jacket; but the panty hose had to remain. I phoned a temporary employment agency and hired my first employee, but unfortunately, he would not be coming for two days and in the afternoon someone vomited in the hallway. Lucky for me the resident manager of the condominiums came by to introduce himself and sent his janitor down to clean up the mess.

That was one of the first lessons I learned in property management: networking will save you more often than your bosses will in times of trouble.

My first employee came on board two days later and he seemed to be a good worker, constantly cleaning, dusting, and emptying those trashcans. Regrettably, while he appeared to be hardworking, he enjoyed sniffing glue during his off hours and kept missing his bus or forgetting the address of where he worked. Although I didn't know much, I knew that if I showed up every day on time, was friendly, and learned my way around, that I could make the job work.

My biggest problem was the sump pumps. The commercial unit housing the retail stores and restaurants was situated below sea level and every day at four o'clock I had to manually run the pumps so the downstairs parking lot and tenants would not have water seeping into their stalls. On weekends the resident manager of the condominiums had his security staff clear the pumps but it took almost a year for everything to be rewired so that the pumps automatically kicked in without human help.

There were other issues with the building; on occasion, the elevator wouldn't open and passengers would be trapped inside; the lights would go on and off at will because of crossed wiring; the plumbing would back up because some sub-contractor had poured left-over grout down the toilet.

It took about two years to resolve all the construction problems and I now understand this is common with new buildings. But, the good news was, I was managing the center. Repairs were getting done and it felt like I was doing something of value. After I had been on the job for about three months, Barbara, the editor of "The Waikiki Beach Press," the weekly newspaper, which was started in 1955 for residents and businesses in Waikiki, came by my office to interview me.

It was a warm day and the room was stifling as we sat in my office surrounded by mops and cleaning supplies. I had a small fan on at full speed moving the air and odor around. Barbara talked about the paper and asked me questions about myself.

"So I heard you are 23 years old?"

"Yes, I am."

"You look like you're 16 with that baby face of yours."

"Thank you, my father's side of the family."

"I did some checking and it appears that you are currently the youngest shopping center manager in America. What do you think about that? You must be very proud of yourself?"

As we sat in my broom closet, with no air conditioning, praying the stench of my sweat did not make it to her nose, I was anything but proud. "Really, I know my mother will be very pleased when I tell her tonight."

My picture and story were on the front page of the Press the following week and I thought everyone at the main office would be excited for me. That was not the case. Little did I know then, the proverbial "poop" was about to hit the fan.

CHAPTER TEN

Press Hound

What I thought would be exciting for everyone at the shopping center and Hawaii Management, was instead, a total disaster…for me, anyway. Everyone, particularly the secretaries, thought I was a "press hound" hoping to make myself appear more important than the company.

It was another lesson I learned: when you work for someone else, never talk to the press without your superior's approval. I later realized it's not because they are afraid of what you might say, but because when you make public appearances or statements, you pull the focus away from the senior staff, and large egos are all a part of the game of business.

I was called in and thoroughly chewed out by Henry and told if I ever talked to the press again I would be immediately fired for cause, plain and simple. Furthermore, this action showed I was not capable of being independent and I would now have a direct supervisor. I would report to him from this moment on so there would be no "mistakes" made in the future.

I was told to wait for my new supervisor outside Henry's office and to stand by the file cabinets, which were in the middle of the room. There were no chairs to sit on and no one offered me one.

Henry's office was directly adjacent to the secretaries' pool and the four of them glared at me as I left. I could hear Gwendolyn,* the head of the pool, and Henry's personal assistant, say distinctly under her breath, just loud enough for me to hear, "You disgusting little twit."

Gwendolyn was in her mid-sixties…trim, medium height, with brilliant white hair and piercing blue eyes… very old school, and ferociously loyal to Henry. After she and her husband moved to Hawaii from the Midwest to escape the cold weather, she came to work for Hawaii Management.

Gwen didn't like women supervisors and made no bones about it, usually mentioning this often within earshot of me. She was always formal, keeping her comments to the very minimum of "yes ma'am," or "no ma'am." When she brought coffee for meetings, there were always just enough cups for the men, and one short when it came to me. "Oh, sorry dear, I miscounted again, I'm getting so forgetful, you'll just have to get your own. I'm sure they'll wait to start the meeting," she said on more than one occasion. Knowing they would never wait, she smiled and they would have a good chuckle at my expense, which delighted her no end.

Gwendolyn had the loyalty of her fellow secretaries and they respected her immensely and did whatever she asked them to do. My reports and memorandums often took more than a week to produce because, as Gwendolyn said, "the ladies are way too busy with the other property managers, and since you are not in a senior position, you'll just have to wait your turn."

The wait often got me in trouble, so I was reduced to doing my own filing and most of my typing. Who would have thought that one of the reasons I survived my first year at Hawaii Management was because of my high school typing class at St. Andrew's Priory.

As I waited, the secretaries chuckled among themselves and I knew I was the reason for their amusement. Finally, after thirty minutes, my frustration got the better of me and I said in a voice loud enough for all to hear, "What's so funny?" They all stopped to look at me and Gwendolyn, ever so sweetly said, "Well Dear, we just realized that Allan* will be your new supervisor."

"So, what does that mean?" I asked.

"Well, Allan is a bit odd...pleasant sometimes, but he has one major issue...well, really two...and we've all learned to live with them."

"What are the issues?" I inquired with as much control as I could gather, fear starting to well up in me.

With the most glee I had ever seen in Gwendolyn's eyes, she said, "The first thing is, Allan is always late...never on time for anything. And the second issue," she paused, waiting for suspense to set in, "he has real problems with women in power positions. He doesn't like women who are strong-minded, wear pants, not enough makeup, and talk without asking permission. You know the kind of women I mean," she said with a bit of a smirk as she described me to a tee.

"Yes," she continued, "I would say he really doesn't like them. Strangely though, his wife is a determined lady, very smart, and he just adores her. Maybe, because she's so petite and pretty. We all call him, Captain Bligh," she went on to say.

I could now feel the sweat trickling down my back as foreboding began to set in. "Captain Bligh?" I asked.

"You know, the captain in *Mutiny on the Bounty*." She was now almost glowing. Just as I was about to ask another question, Allan walked into the office.

CHAPTER ELEVEN

Captain Bligh

Allan Gibson,* or "Boomer" to his friends, walked with a swagger, not that he was super-confident, but because of problems with his knees that had plagued him since childhood. He was in constant pain which made him extremely irritable, even on good days. He kept his weight down because it made it easier for him to walk, and also because he abhorred overweight people, particularly women.

Boomer always wore a sports jacket as he felt it presented the right image when dealing with people, but the truth was, he was constantly cold, even in our balmy 85-degree weather. When I shook his hand as he gestured me into his office, it was cold as ice.

His office was an open cubicle, which made it easy for everyone within twenty feet to hear conversations and telephone calls. It was cluttered with books, magazines, jackets, sweaters, dirty coffee mugs and photos, with papers scattered everywhere. Stacks of spreadsheets, management proposals for new centers, corporate policy folders, letters, some in draft form, and others ready for his signature, were strewn across his desk. Clearly, his office was where everything came to be processed before being sent out to supervisors, management and maintenance staff. There was a large note taped to his chair, which read: "Boomer, clean your desk before you go home. Henry".

He removed the note, placed it on his Dictaphone, and sat down. From behind thick, wired-rimmed glasses, the kind John Denver would wear, he stared at me with his small, sharp blue eyes for what seemed an eternity, but was probably only a minute. He alternated between stroking his goatee and running a hand through his thick blonde hair.

Finally, Allan stood up and began to pace, saying, as he looked down at me, "I am here to teach you about management and how to run a shopping center. I will meet you at one o'clock at your office. You are now dismissed." With that, he stalked out of his office and into Henry's, closing the door behind him.

As I sat there hurt and afraid, as I needed this job desperately, I wanted to cry, but remembered another lesson my Dad taught me when I first started working at Chaney. He said working in real estate was like war. "Never show any weakness. If you show you are vulnerable, they will know you are weak and go for the kill. Cry when you're alone, but never let them see weakness." I walked out with my head high and drove to Discovery Bay waiting to see what lay ahead with Boomer.

Allan arrived at 1:20 p.m. and I realized, as Gwendolyn mentioned, punctuality was not one of his major assets. Neither was tact. "Your office stinks," he said as he sat in the chair at my desk, opening and scavenging through the drawers. He found one of my favorite pens, put it in his jacket pocket, and looked at me to see if I would say something. I said nothing as I sat in the guest chair by the door.

I could tell he now felt he had established control over me as he said, "You need to find another place for these supplies and clean this place up."

"I don't have any place for them," I responded.

That was his opportunity, and he began to lecture, "Stephany, if you don't understand, I will explain; but never tell me you can't or you don't have. Figure it out; use your brain. Or are you just too stupid?"

"I am not stupid, Boomer," I replied.

"Do not call me Boomer, that's for my friends and you are not one of them. I am Allan to you. Can that pea brain of yours understand that?" My face turned red from the anger that was taking over from the hurt I felt before, but I simply replied, "Yes."

"Yes, what?" he asked.

"Yes, Allan. I understand that I am to call you Allan," I countered. "Good, now let's walk around."

We toured the Center and he told me what to do; he allowed no questions, he only gave commands. At one point, he chose to take the stairs rather than the elevator. Turning to me he said, "Stephany, I can tell by your weight you're lazy and adverse to exercise, but please try to keep up."

After making the rounds of the shops and restaurants, he proclaimed: "I will be here everyday promptly at 8:00 a.m. and again at 4:30 p.m. and I expect to see progress." With that he departed.

For the next several weeks, Allan came everyday, usually at 8:45 a.m. and again at 5:00 p.m., always critical of my progress. Then one day he showed up in a particularly foul mood, and on our daily walk around the Mall he stopped suddenly and exclaimed, "What's this?" He had found a layer of dust on the windowsill by the elevator. He slid his index finger across the sill, scooping up a bunch of dust, and stuck it right under my nose. "Do you know what this is?"

"Dust," I replied.

This incensed him. "Stephany," he said in a stern voice, "Obliviously you haven't learned a thing I have been teaching you over these months. I guess you're just too stupid and lazy to understand. If you can't understand, you need to quit this job. You need to quit now if you can't handle simple tasks."

Looking at him, with his finger still between us, I said, "I need this job."

"Need and want are two different things; you have to want this job to make it work," he growled. He took out his handkerchief, wiped the dirt off his finger saying, "I want you to keep a log of everything you do every minute of the day while you are still employed here. We will go over it daily. You need to learn the basics, if your pea brain can comprehend them."

For the next two months, I kept the log, writing everything down from conversations with tenants, to meetings, to what I had for lunch. Allan had his secretary page me every 30 minutes, asking where I was and what I was doing at the moment. If I didn't answer within five minutes, Allan himself would call and read me the riot act.

One afternoon, the architect of the McDonald's restaurant invited me to lunch at Victoria Station, across the street from Discovery Bay. Unfortunately, I mentioned this to Allan's secretary and during the meal I received nine pages within forty-five minutes from my "electronic leash." Each time I had to get up from the table and go to the manager's station to return the call. Each time I answered, she said, "Sorry, I was looking for a file, but I found it. Thank you for returning my call." The architect ate lunch almost completely alone, and I ended up taking mine home for dinner.

When I saw Allan that afternoon, he looked at me with a smirk on his face and said, "Did you enjoy your lunch at Victoria Station? I hear the food is excellent." I said nothing.

Allan continued to come to my office and grill me everyday about everything that occurred. "Were you polite? What did you say to the tenants? I heard otherwise. Why did you do it this way and not that way? Why did you eat that? It puts on weight and you're too fat as it is," were his constant comments and questions.

One Thursday afternoon he was reading my log and queried, "Where were you from 3:00 p.m. to 3:20 p.m.? There's nothing listed here." "I was in the bathroom." "What took you so long, were you doing drugs?" he demanded. Something inside me snapped and I looked straight at him and said, "I don't do drugs. I had a sour stomach that day, and I do NOT appreciate you questioning me in that tone."

For the first time since he became my supervisor, Allan smiled. He closed the log and said in a frigid voice, "Alright Stephany, we will chat with Henry about this tomorrow.

He left and I knew I was in trouble, but this time I didn't care. If they fire me, they fire me, I thought, but I've had enough! Anger replaced fear and I concluded there and then that no job was worth the humiliation I had been enduring on a daily basis for almost a year.

CHAPTER TWELVE

The Mutiny Of The Secretaries

Tomorrow arrived and I was at the main office at my scheduled time of 1:00 p.m. Allan was late as usual and Henry was in a meeting in his office with the door closed. I was busy filing my logs. The secretaries had long ago stopped doing anything for me and filing was now a regular part of my job.

Allan stomped into the office and he was livid. He exploded as he came up to me, "Stephany, I just came from a meeting with Freddy,* the manager of the grocery mart at the center, and he said you did not get him the information on time for the loading hours and some of his merchandise spoiled because he was not able to schedule his team. He lost a substantial amount of money because of you!"

"I did get him the information," I countered.

"Stephany, the manger is my wife's cousin, a part of my family. Are you saying one of my own relatives is lying to me? Are you telling me that he is lying?" At this point, Allan was practically screaming. Everyone in the office was frozen.

"I did give him the information, Allan. I have it right here," I said as I went directly to the file and pulled out the confirmation form showing the stamped date and time I had personally delivered it, which was exactly a week before the alleged problem occurred.

"How do I know this is true? For all I know you could have had one of the secretaries place it here to cover your butt. You women all cover up for each other! That's what you folks do to protect your incompetence and stupidity."

"I do my own filing, Allan. The secretaries had nothing to do with this. I delivered the information to Freddy's assistant myself," my voice quivered in anger as I answered. "So now you are saying, my cousin's assistant is the liar?" "Allan, I am not saying any such thing."

"I'm going back to the center and check with Freddy's assistant and if I find that you lied, I will fire your fat ass immediately and you will never work in property management again. Do you understand me? Do you want to change your story now before I leave here? Do you understand me?"

"I understand, I didn't lie," I spouted, looking directly at him.

At this point, Henry came out of his office because he could hear Allan's yelling and said, "What's the matter?" Allan looked at all of us and said in a calm, controlled voice that everything was fine and he would be back in an hour. He placed the file under his arm and left for the shopping center. Henry shrugged and went back to his meeting.

I was angry, but Gwendolyn was bursting mad. I could have sworn steam was coming out of her ears as she nearly shouted, "What did he say about us? How dare he talk that way!" she turned to the others. They were visibly upset and talking among themselves. I couldn't hear what they were saying, but I knew they were furious.

I went into the lunchroom and made myself a cup of coffee and waited for Allan to return. After about ten minutes, Gwendolyn and Sandy,* Allan's secretary, came in and sat down. Sandy was of Japanese ancestry; both parents had met and married at the sugar plantation on Kauai before World War II. She was small in stature, about thirty-five and very timid by nature. She married her high school boyfriend, and being Allan's assistant had been the biggest job of her life, and by far the most stressful. Around the office she was called "Mrs. Rolaids" because she was constantly eating them as her stomach hurt everyday since she began working with Allan.

"He shouldn't have spoken to you like that in front of us," Gwendolyn began.

"That's how he always talks to me."

"That's not right, very insulting," Sandy chirped. "Now why would you both care at this point," I said, looking out the window. When I turned, I noticed Gwendolyn looking at me with softness in her eyes I had never seen before, saying, "We all have limits, Stephany, and Allan stepped out of bounds today. I know you were telling the truth," she went on.

I stared at her and said, "And how do you know that?"

"I have Sandy check your files everyday to make sure everything is logged correctly."

Gwendolyn stood and said, "Stephany, come back to the main room and wait for Allan. I believe everything will be alright now."

I didn't understand what she meant, but knew not to ask any questions. The three of us returned to the main office where the files were located. The other two secretaries were scurrying about moving papers from one file to another, then logging them to make sure they knew where each paper was. Sandy went into Allan's office and removed his Dictaphone tape and replaced it with another one. She then threw the old one into the trash and covered it up with paper.

Allan came back about fifteen minutes later, said nothing to me, and tossed the file on Sandy's desk. There was no discussion or apology. He didn't even look at me. I knew Freddy's assistant had told him the truth about the memorandum, but I still didn't know what was next in store for me.

As he stood there, Gwendolyn began ever so sweetly, "Allan, the girls and I know how busy you are these days."

"Very busy, too busy," he mumbled.

"Why don't you let us work with Stephany and we can train her for the skills she really needs here, like filing, typing, sorting paperwork, and processing accounting forms."

Allan perked up with this welcome offer.

Just then, Henry opened his door and Allan repeated the offer from the secretaries. "What do you think?" he asked Henry.

Henry took a few moments to consider the suggestion before responding. "It could work. Gwendolyn, you work with her and that will help free up Allan's time. Allan, you continue to supervise her, but you don't have to now go down to the center everyday. She can come here". "Everyone agree?" One and all, including me, nodded their head.

From that moment on, life changed for the better. Over the next four months, the secretaries met with me daily and taught me how to do the paperwork. They even gave me old accounting files so I could write my budgets and got Miriam* in Accounting to tutor me. My budgets were outstanding. Even Henry commented how good they were for a first year manager. My letters were immediately typed and processed, and when no other managers were around, they took dictation from me. Gwendolyn was the fastest as she was an expert in shorthand. They even paged me when Allan or Henry was coming down to the center for a surprise visit so I would be prepared.

As life got easier, Allan's literally became a living hell. All his files had papers missing or were mixed up in different files and he couldn't find anything in his office. Some documents were found under his sweaters, and once, even his expense account went to Alan Beall's office instead of Henry's, much to his embarrassment and Henry's displeasure when Alan questioned the reimbursement requests. Allan swore he dictated several letters daily, but often when he went to replay the Dictaphone after lunch, there was nothing on them. He even had the old machine replaced, and still recordings were lost. He got so far behind in his work that his temper flared frequently and his personality became overly confrontational. He would come into the secretaries' area on a weekly basis accusing and screaming, "What the hell is going on here? Where are my files? Who is tampering with my Dictaphone?"

Gwendolyn would look at him with a stern face and speak like a mother to a misbehaving son, "Allan, what are you talking about?" She would then go to the file and show him everything was in prefect order. She would bring him his dictated letters. "You dropped these off last week. Don't you remember?"

Allan would storm back into his cubicle and silently brood for the rest of the day. I was often around during these outbursts, and after he left, everyone would look at each other and smile. Gwendolyn would look at me and wink.

The Gaslight treatment was in full force and working well. After four months, Allan was so stressed out that Henry became concerned and asked him to take a vacation and he willingly agreed. Before he left for a holiday in California, he, Henry, and I met in Henry's office and Henry said that I had done so much better under Allan's leadership that I was to be transferred to a new assignment. Allan said nothing. Henry said, that while it was a lateral transfer, it was considered a promotion and he was to become my supervisor again. I was now the new on-site property manager and leasing agent for the Honolulu Merchandise Mart. It was a new start and I was excited. I would still be around the main office, but not as much. The secretaries had taught me what to do and how to succeed in property management. They were my protectors and had saved me from disaster.

It was another lesson I learned in my career. Never, never, never insult or upset the secretaries. They are the Rulers of the Realm. They control the flow of paper, they rule the appointment calendars, phone messages, and they know where everything is located. To cross them is to sign your own death warrant.

To this day, when meeting new people, I always make it a point to say "hello" to the secretaries and have a conversation with them. They set the rules and I always adhere to them. I would not have survived without their intervention, and although they usually work the hardest in every business transaction, they often get the least compensation. Secretaries will always have my loyalty and my utmost respect.

CHAPTER THIRTEEN

John Waynes Vs. Matt Dillons

In the world of real estate, both residential and commercial, there are two separate and unequal groups: leasing/sales agents and property managers. The leasing/sales agents are the John Waynes, often full of swagger and bravado. The property managers are the Matt Dillons, often lacking confidence, suspicious, and cautious of everyone.

Another analogy would be to say the leasing/sales agents are the movie stars, while the property managers are the stagehands. They are treated differently in all repects, from the type of office they get, what their pay and bonus structures are, and most importantly, their social strata in the world of real estate.

Leasing/sales agents get all the glory because they bring home the bacon for the company; big commissions come to them that succeed. As for the property managers who manage the leases, rentals, and accounting for the company, they get the scraps and are often the brunt of jokes. The two types of real estate professionals dress dissimilarly, carry themselves in a different way, and almost always drive totally different types of cars.

You can tell the two groups apart when you first meet them because of their physical appearance. The leasing/sales agent is almost always perfectly groomed…silk or linen, Prada, St. John, Chanel, Coach, Bally shoes and briefcases. Their cars are usually Mercedes, Lexus, Jaguar, BMW, and the ever-classy Porsche.

What is the classic real estate agent joke? What's the difference between a porcupine and a real estate agent driving a Porsche? The answer: with the porcupine, the pricks are on the outside.

Sales are ninety-five percent about perception and image and sales/leasing agents work this angle to the core. Personal fitness trainers and clubs are a must to keep the "look" going. They are about making the client "feel good" about spending money, whether it's for a house, office building, retail space, or investment.

Clothes and shoes are some of their biggest investments. In Boston and New York, they gravitate to Boss, Prada, and Gucci. In Los Angeles and Honolulu, they wear silk Tommy Bahama or Tori Richards aloha shirts, while Reyns wear is left for the bankers and insurance people. Gucci, Cole Haan, or Ferragamo loafers are usually their shoes of choice, of course without socks. In Texas everyone wears cowboy boots, but the John Waynes' are almost always made of alligator, snakeskin, or ostrich.

The property managers, or Matt Dillons, on the other hand, are a stark contrast. Many are older, retired military. If they're younger, they're usually not dapper and don't enjoy working the art of the deal. Selling or leasing is not their game, but they still want to be in real estate. As a property manager, they can command their own ship.

The property manager's favorite material is polyester or cotton-polyester-mix because it's washable and takes very little ironing. Pants or skirts are usually an inch or more too short, probably from too many washings, and they love Macy's aloha shirts or blouses. The shirts do not have to be tucked in because comfort takes precedence over style. They love Florsheim shoes or boots because they can be resoled. Their cars of choice are soccer-mom mini vans, American SUVs, or Toyota Camrys. Their exercise is driving from property to property, walking up and down stairs, and constantly searching for resident managers and maintenance staff that say they are on property but are usually somewhere else.

While the sales/leasing people focus on schmoozing, property managers are fixed on keeping everything running smoothly so they can have a quiet, uninterrupted meal. Many are chronically exhausted because they often work more the sixty hours a week. Their workload includes all the paperwork for each property and getting called in the middle of the night because of maintenance problems. Property managers are usually required to attend association meetings, which Boards of Directors frequently use as a social hour with the neighbors as the managers sit and wait patiently to get important projects approved.

As the new property supervisor of the Honolulu Merchandise Mart, I was to be both the leasing agent and property manager for the project and would have to walk a thin line between the two. I needed to be both a John Wayne and a Matt Dillon, and very few people had been successful at both. I was required to attend certain functions as a leasing agent, but did not have the clothes, style, or knowledge of how it all worked. I also had to be on call to take care of the problems a property and its tenants are faced with on a daily basis.

An example of how these groups viewed each was told to me a couple of years ago by a property manager of one of the largest commercial leasing and property management companies in Hawaii. It seemed the young male leasing agents, when they got hungry in the late mornings, which was almost daily because of their constant physical workouts, would often come into the company's lunchroom and take the property mangers' lunch. This routine particularly irked the managers because the agents' average pay was about four times more than theirs.

One Friday morning before the start of a long weekend, two of the managers walked into the lunchroom and caught three agents taking their food again, and when confronted, one of the agents took out a $5 bill from his wallet, threw it down on the lunch table and said, "This should pay for the sandwich and your time getting it for me. Thanks for lunch." The agents all laughed and started to walk out of the room.

One of the property managers, who was about twenty-five years older, a retired military officer who had served twenty years in the Army including a tour in Iraq, walked up to them. He was six inches shorter and thirty pounds heavier, and as he approached the younger and taller agent, he said, "Wait, I have something else for you." With this comment, he laid out a quick upper cut and punched the egotistical agent square in the nose, knocking him down to the floor and spattering blood all over his brand new Polo long-sleeved white dress shirt and sky-blue Boss tie.

The others in the room didn't move a muscle. As the agent sat on the floor holding his broken nose and moaning, the property manager looked down, and as he stepped over him to walk out the door said, "That's my tip."

The good news is that no one was fired that day and the lunches stopped disappearing.

CHAPTER FOURTEEN

The Tricks Of The Trade

Some of the perks of property management are attending lunches and seminars. If you're just beginning your career, they give you an opportunity to meet new people and make connections. The company pays for your lunch or your tuition, and you get to be away from the mundane day-to-day grind and the constant complaints of tenants and bosses. Upper management requires junior managers to attend these functions. That way senior managers can gain information without spending several hours sitting at boring meetings listening to someone drone on about the latest cleaning techniques, or how fabulous someone was in that so-called marathon leasing transaction that made hundreds of thousands of dollars for the leasing agents.

In my second year as a property manager, I attended an all-day seminar. At lunch I sat beside a property manager named Kraig Woo.*

I had seen him at every seminar or luncheon I attended and he knew who I was and where I worked.

Kraig was 32 years old, of average height, pale, and extremely thin, which I attributed to his constant chain smoking. His fingertips were yellow from nicotine. He had a plain face with tiny wrinkles around his mouth, which made him look older than his years.

Kraig always appeared antsy, constantly twitching and moving in his chair, or shifting his stance when he was standing. He was a middle manager, an assistant vice president for one of the top property management companies in town. Kraig had been with for the company for about ten years, ever since graduating from the University of Hawaii as an accounting major. What set him apart from other property managers was that he was always impeccably attired.

Kraig wore fine silk or handmade linen shirts and trousers from Andy Mohan, the most expensive tailor in Honolulu. His ties were Givenchy, his shoes Gucci. His hair was perfectly trimmed and his car was an immaculate, late-model Mercedes.

After table chitchat and the rubber chicken for which the Sheraton Waikiki was famous, everyone left but Craig and I. As we sat there, finishing our coffee, I looked at him and blurted out, "So how do you do it?"

"Excuse me?" he replied.

"So how do you do it? Beautiful car, clothes, shoes…are you a trust fund baby?" I said.

"No way!" He chuckled at the thought of himself, the son of a poor immigrant butcher at Oahu Market and a maid at Outrigger Hotels having a trust fund.

"Seriously, I know you don't make that much money. Do you get overrides from the listing agents?" I asked.

He looked at me for a moment, as if he were sizing up my motives and, as he sipped his coffee, simply said, "Well, it's not as clandestine as you might think. Amway," he said.

"What are you talking about?" I inquired, puzzled at his answer.

"It's Amway. Network marketing."

Realizing I was young and ignorant, but very interested in learning the ways of property management, he instinctively knew I was not someone who could hurt his position. So he began talking.

"As a building manager, you write up the budget for the property. Your supervisor and the owner of the property then approve it. The budget always has categories for janitorial supplies, repairs and maintenance. The supplies can come from anyone as long as they are within or below budget. If you or a family member creates a small business with a different name, then who's to know that the company you are using is, in fact, your own business that provides supplies to the building?"

"Isn't that unethical?" I said.

"How is it unethical? Who are you hurting? You're within budget and often below budget, your supplies are delivered on time, and the products are good. Your supervisor is happy, the owner is happy, and the tenants are happy. And the best part is, you make an average of $250 more a month per property…and it's all legal. I'm in charge of four buildings. That's another $1,000 a month in my pocket."

Kraig leaned back in his chair and continued, "Now when it comes to repairs and maintenance, that's a little trickier because you have to sign purchase orders which authorize direct payments to your company."

"So how does that work," I asked, totally intrigued.

"All you need to do is to create another company. Find

yourself a couple of good handymen. They're worth their weight in gold. Handymen usually cost between $25 and $30 an hour and they can paint, do carpentry, lay tile, fix toilets, and usually know how to do basic electrical repairs. You then create your own little company. Say you call it Acme Maintenance, and you hire these two guys to work for you on call. Whenever there is a need for repairs or maintenance, you call Acme," he continued. "The repair and maintenance category usually is budgeted at $75 an hour to cover real emergencies when you need licensed plumbers or electricians, but usually a handyman is all you need. So Acme charges your property $50 to $60 per hour and your little company makes a $25 to $30 an hour profit, and no one knows but you. That's probably another $300 to $500 a month for you, per property. Again, you're using legitimate workers and getting the job done. And because you have a vested interest in your little company, you make darn sure your boys do a good job."

Kraig was now on a roll and very intent in continuing the conversation. He had found someone interested in what he had to say and I was a sponge. Our conversation lasted another forty-five minutes with both of us missing the early afternoon group discussion on "Marketing Your Property."

"Now here's another way to make additional income for property managers, but I wouldn't recommend it. If you get caught, you will be instantly fired, but the money is so easy, many managers just can't resist doing it."

"Okay, this sounds interesting, what?" I asked, completely absorbed in his fascinating revelations.

"Well, every budget has a vacancy rate factored into it, right?"

I nodded.

"And the average rates are between 5 and 10 percent, depending on the property, location, condition, etc. With me so far?"

Again, I nodded.

"So, as an example, take an apartment building of thirty units. It normally will have one to three empty units at any given time. Some managers will rent one or two of those supposedly empty units for cash discounts. A case in point: a one-bedroom apartment in Waikiki rents for $1,000 a month, and the manager will do a cash rental of $750 and pocket the money. Many folks don't use checks and prefer to pay with cash because they know that some property managers will give them a discount; the paperwork is the same, but it's never processed. The tenants never know they are occupying the unit illegally; they pay their rent on time and have the same status as everyone else. The owners don't know anything is amiss because you are on budget. The manager makes $750 cash which goes directly into his or her pocket each month, without anyone knowing."

"Wow, incredible," I gasped. "That's more than I take home each month!"

"In the commercial arena, it's harder to do because retail is too visible and people pay with checks. However, with smaller warehouses and office buildings, managers can often get away with it. Tell me how many owners walk through their buildings and compare rental income against the number of offices leased?"

"I wouldn't have a clue." I shrugged.

"Zero to one percent," he estimated.

"The only time managers get caught is when an owner comes to the property and tries to match his rent rolls, but this is very rare. Usually the manager gets around the question by saying he is repairing another unit and had the tenants temporarily move into the supposedly empty space," he continued. "So getting caught is very uncommon because owners are usually too busy with their other businesses and just want to make budget or below. They don't pay attention to details. They leave those to their managers," he said, smiling ever so slightly as he sipped the last of his coffee.

"As I said, it's very lucrative and you can become wealthy off your clients without them ever knowing, but if you do get caught it would be the end of your career in this business," he stated firmly as we rose and moved along to the next session.

His final comments were of caution. "Remember that if the bosses want someone new to do the repairs and maintenance work, it's probably because they are affiliated with them so don't put up a fuss. Let them come in, be patient, and in time, work your guys back onto the property. There are enough coins to go around and the owners, for the most part, don't really care who does the work as long as it gets done properly."

With that last comment, Kraig and I parted company. About a year later, I heard he had left his company and started his own real estate property management business, specializing in vacation rentals.

When I ran into him one day he told me, "The owners are all absentees, they always let you know when they are coming over, the cleaning fees are exorbitant, and the extra money is so easy."

Whenever I see Kraig around town these days, he tells me his company is thriving. He is still rail-thin, chain smoking, and married with two grown daughters; one is a medical doctor and the other, a corporate attorney. "Not bad for the son of a butcher and a maid," he says to me.

As for his advice, I never got into the "network marketing business" or the "temporary cash rental business." I have always thought it was a bit morally corrupt, if not totally illegal.

It must be said over the years that I have found most property management companies and managers straight up and honorable.

However, I do know there are some property managers today who willingly use these devious methods to increase their income. This sort of activity will continue as long as owners take a passive roll in the management of their properties.

If the cookie jar is open, and no one is around to see, the temptation of taking a cookie or two is too strong for many, and like a mom, owners need to inspect from time to time or face an empty jar.

CHAPTER FIFTEEN

The Honolulu Merchandise Mart

The Honolulu Merchandise Mart, originally built in 1908 as a branch of the Young Men's Christian Association, was one of the most beautiful buildings in its heyday, with a stone, neo-classical facade, grand staircases of marble, guest rooms, a huge ballroom, an Olympic sized swimming pool, and squash and handball courts.

It was a place where young gentlemen, particularly those in the military, spent a good part of their free time. Activities included swimming and dancing lessons, refinement classes, and a cotillion for these young men new to the adult world.

Friday nights were especially enjoyable when the eligible young ladies of Honolulu put on make-up, did their hair just right, got dressed in their finest dresses or *mu'umu'u*, and came to dance to the latest Hawaiian jazz bands. They were thrilled to socialize with these clean-cut, well- starched gentlemen in their crisp uniforms and newly shined shoes. It's been said that many romances blossomed there during those festive evenings.

The YMCA flourished until 1946 when it was sold to an entrepreneur from the mainland who decided that what Honolulu needed was a merchandise mart. The YMCA moved its operations to another location across the street. The new owner installed two elevators and built an additional floor on the west, or Ewa, side of the building. It soon became one of the leading office buildings in Honolulu, and with its modern conveniences, flourished for the next fourteen years.

In 1960, the Honolulu Merchandise Mart went through another renovation when it got a new façade. Plaster and concrete covered the original exterior, making it more functional. The grand staircases were divided into two entrances. Walls were erected to create retail and office space. The grand ballroom and swimming pool were replaced with storage rooms and lockers, providing additional income. The old boarding rooms were turned into 110 small offices, and the downstairs area renovated to accommodate five retail and restaurant spaces.

In the fall of 1978, when I first walked into the Honolulu Merchandise Mart, it had been over eighteen years since the last renovation. The building had fallen on hard times and much of "The Mart," as it was known around Honolulu, was termite eaten, had exposed wiring everywhere, and was filthy dirty. The fire escapes, entry doors, and offices appeared to have been in a time warp. When walking the hallways, it felt like you had gone back in time to another era. For the first few months I felt like Christopher Reeve's character in "Somewhere in Time," never really knowing what lay ahead or where I would end up when I went down a dark corridor.

With the cheap rent, in comparison to the rest of downtown, the tenants, as tactfully as I can say, were an eclectic bunch. The building was home to political action groups, a crack seed store, magic shop, clothing designer and manufacturer, restaurant, jeweler, sail maker, printer, interior designer, architect, urban planner, bondsman, auctioneer, artist, past and present state legislators, attorneys, insurance agents, and an array of young and old talent just starting or ending their careers. One hundred fifteen different tenants, each with his or her particular personality and agenda, occupied the spaces and two of the most interesting were Pigeon Man and The Bookworm.

PIGEON MAN

When I arrived, Pigeon Man, who acquired his name because of the prey he lived on, had been living illegally in one of the storage rooms below the old swimming pool for about three years. He was very elusive, constantly moving from room to room, always one step away from being nabbed.

Pigeon Man never came out until dark, like the vampires of ancient tales, when he would hunt for pigeons to eat. He wore black trousers, shirt, and hat. When we caught a glimpse of him, his face was always covered with a surgeon's mask. There were many afternoons when I felt an eerie sensation of being watched from inside the walls of the corridors. Although my janitor and I often searched but never found him, we could certainly smell him.

My other employee was the maintenance man for the building. Ricardo* was a no-nonsense Puerto Rican fellow, a former Marine, 45 years old. He had come to Hawaii via the Vietnam War and his job at the Mart was something he loved, mainly because he had the freedom to work at his own pace and hours, which was vastly different from his life in the military.

Ricardo hated Pigeon Man with a passion, largely because he was constantly cleaning or repairing things that Pigeon Man had soiled or damaged. I often found the janitor and Ricardo cleaning up the blood, guts, and plucked feathers of a recently killed bird Pigeon Man had eaten the night before.

Ricardo and I finally cornered him one Friday evening when he started a fire on one of the wooden balconies to roast a freshly caught pigeon. I called the fire department, which quickly responded, but in the confusion caused by the firemen running around, and Pigeon Man trying to grab his now-cooked dinner and escape, Ricardo and I ambushed him on the balcony with chairs and a broomstick. Trapped, he started wailing and moaning like a wild animal. When the police arrested him and removed his mask, his face was hideous…severely disfigured with deep pockmarks and scars.

For a moment, I actually felt sorry for him, but it was fleeting, as the building had no fire alarms or sprinklers, his freaky act had caused a fire that could have burned down the building and killed a lot of people.

THE BOOKWORM

The Bookworm was a legal tenant for many years on a month-to-month lease at the Mart. He was a smallish, chubby Asian man in his middle 50's who had never worked and lived with his mother all his life. His office space was about 80 square feet, about the size of a small child's bedroom. It had books everywhere, some stacked to the top of the ten foot ceiling. His favorite reading material consisted of manuscripts on witchcraft and the occult.

The Bookworm also dressed in dark colors and wore an overcoat, which was very unusual in Hawaii's 85-degree weather. His appearance was all the more peculiar because of the dark glasses he wore, even at night, and he spoke only in singsong rhymes.

At first, he was a pleasant little oddity, coming into my office every afternoon to chat, but then he started bringing me gifts of flowers, candy, and pictures of moonlight beaches.

One day, when the Bookworm was sitting in my office, my boyfriend dropped by, came over to my desk, and gave me a little kiss. The Bookworm immediately became agitated and left before I could introduce them.

The following week, he came into my office for our daily chats, but now would stare at me and begin his rhymes without answering my questions.

On Friday, he began, "The slut is a mutt and needs to be cut."

"Excuse me", I said, looking up from my paperwork.

"The mutt is a slut and needs to be cut."

Now I put my pen down and looked directly at him. "What did you just say to me?"

"The whore is a bore, and not of the lore. Someone who lies needs to die. The slut is a mutt and needs to be cut."

"Okay, that's enough! Get out, don't come back!" My voice was angry as I snarled at him.

He rose and began to raise his voice, "The slut is a mutt and needs to be cut! The mutt is a slut and needs to be cut!"

"Get out now or you are going to jail," I screamed back.

The word "jail" brought him back to earth and he quickly left. I locked the door and called Ricardo to come up to my office. When he arrived, I told him what had happened. He listened intently and said, "Don't worry, I'll take care of him." I wrote up the Bookworm's cancellation of lease and gave it to Ricardo: a tenant had thirty days to move after being terminated.

Ricardo escorted me to my car and said, "Take the weekend off and don't come around here." When I came to work on Monday, the Bookworm was gone and his office had been cleaned and painted.

"What happened?"

"Nothing. He decided it was in his best interests to move out sooner than later. He won't be bothering the Mart or you again," Ricardo said with a knowing smile.

Both Pigeon Man and the Bookworm never came back to the property, and I will be the first to tell you, I was elated when these two characters left. I am not an anxious or nervous person by nature, but these two really gave me the heebie-jeebies, and for many months afterwards I was constantly looking over my shoulder and jumping at the slightest sound.

And it was here, in this haven for the strangest of the strange, I met the most beautiful man in the world.

CHAPTER SIXTEEN

The Most Beautiful Man In The World

Before you get acquainted with the most beautiful man in the world, you need to know a little more about my background and me. I'm an Orthodox Christian of Greek descent. Orthodox are often called Eastern Catholics, but we are more traditional and old school. "Ortho" comes from the Greek word for "straight," "upright," or "correct." Orthodox believe their faith is the most direct way to God. Many of our traditions are from the Byzantine era and have not changed in centuries.

As a young girl, I learned Catholics fasted on Fridays, Orthodox on Wednesdays and Fridays. While Catholics say confession anonymously in a confessional, we go to the priest's office, look at him directly while kneeling on the floor, and ask for forgiveness. I was taught you didn't enter into marriage lightly, because divorce was not an option and you were married until death. His Eminence, Archbishop Iakovos, who was the head of the Greek Orthodox Archdiocese of North and South America until the late 1990's, knew me by my first name.

Good Friday is our day of atonement, and if possible, we spent from noon until 3:00 p.m., which is said to be Jesus' time of suffering on the cross, at church praying and asking God to forgive our transgressions.

When I graduated from Holy Nativity School, I received the Best Christian of the School award for exemplifying the true value of Christ's teachings.

I also spent seven years at St. Andrew's Priory where I was essentially reared by the Episcopal nuns and teachers. They were warm and nurturing and there were moments in my life when I thought about life in a convent. Particularly after hearing that only one girl had ever gone on to the nunnery from our school and her name was Sister Stephanie. (Class of 1941.) Was it divine intervention, I more than once thought, during those years? I recited the Angelus daily, attended chapel at the Priory five days a week, and Greek Orthodox Church for three hours on Sunday. Some of my classmates teased me and called me "Sinless Sofos."

However, when I discovered boys in my junior year of high school and got to interact and hang with them in our Speedos at daily swim practice at the Iolani School pool, those thoughts quickly disappeared.

In college, I tried to reject my upbringing and religious education and I partied like a rock star…surfing, playing tennis, enjoying the boys, and discovering all the things one does at a university. Life was good, but over time I kept drifting back to church and realized no matter how hard I tried, I could not give up my early beliefs.

By the time I was working in real estate, I was not the fundamentalist of my youth, but I had come back to many of my traditional old-fashioned viewpoints where certain ideas and prejudices about people and their lifestyles were very black and white. There was extremely little gray in my thought process, and as you may have guessed, although I had been on my own for a few years, I was still very conservative.

The first time I met Jeffery Edward Sousa or "Theresa," as he preferred to be called, it was late in the afternoon and he was standing at the top of the former grand staircase at the entrance to the Merchandise Mart. His blond hair flowed past his shoulders and his eyes were the bluest of blue, enhanced with a bit of eyeliner. He was six feet two inches tall, fashionably thin, and wore tight blue jeans, an equally tight white T-shirt, and white, open-toed sandals. Standing there, he seemed to glow, and appeared almost larger than life.

"You must be Stephany! I'm Theresa, but my friends call me Terry. I've heard all about you," he said as he looked down at me. He proceeded to prance down the stairs and held his hand out to give me a handshake and a little peck on the cheek.

"I work at Summer Breeze,* and I help cut the material and sometimes model for them," he said with a giggle.

He continued to chat and chirp non-stop for another five minutes, all the while scanning my outfit of brown polyester slacks, brown pumps, beige linen jacket, and my ever present polyester long sleeve white blouse with matching bouffant tie.

Finally, he stopped, looked at me with his piercing eyes and sighed. I could swear he was reading my mind.

"Hmmm, very straight laced, aren't we?" he mused.

Not waiting for my reply, he gave me a big smile with his brilliant white teeth, pulled his hair into a ponytail, and said,

"Oh my, gotta to go. See you soon."

With that, he waved and climbed the steps of the grand staircase two at a time and was gone. I thought I saw a tear forming in his eye, but he was moving too fast for me to see clearly.

George, the owner of "Jiyoji," our little restaurant in the Mart, which served breakfast Monday through Friday and lunch from 6:00 a.m. to 2:00 p.m. daily to the hungry downtown office workers at dirt cheap prices had watched my encounter with Terry and was chuckling as I turned and looked at him.

George had served thirty years in the Army, the last fifteen as a Sergeant First Class, training troops in Asia. He was compact and fit, which was surprising with all the beer he drank. He had married a Japanese national and moved to Hawaii to retire because his family in Indiana did not appreciate his ethnic choice for a wife. His personal philosophy was "live and let live, because in the blink of an eye you can be sent to war."

George started the restaurant to give himself something to do because he was bored, liked to cook, and his wife couldn't stand his drinking and watching television at home any longer.

"Was he what I think he was?" I said.

George was popping open the first of ten beers he averaged after work, took a big swallow, smiled and said, "Well if you're thinking *mahu,* you're right. Theresa, or 'Princess,' as I call him, is our resident transvestite."

Back in the 1970s, transgender individuals in the United States were often thought of as garbage. Sodomy and homosexuality were punishable by prison time, the medical profession deemed them mentally disturbed, and Christians believed them to be mortal sinners. It was difficult for them to get jobs, and, as Terry discovered, practically the only avenue of employment was the oldest profession in the world...prostitution.

Even so, Hawaii's culture is more understanding. The ancient Hawaiians believed all people possess both male and female traits or duel souls. Their culture accepts transsexuals, or *mahu,* as they are known, and historically, many *mahu* are embraced by the community.

Knowing this, Terry had come to Hawaii from California a couple of years before I met him to find a life because he could no longer tolerate his family's judgment. Yet even though there was more tolerance in Hawaii, there still was a great deal of bigotry.

After we got acquainted, Terry would stop by my office for a weekly chat. The truth was, he would talk and I would listen. He was charming, witty and smart, and I would have none of it. I'd just sit there reading the paper or stoically watching the clock on my desk.

Other tenants would come by my office and joke about our resident "faggot" or "hooker." My term of endearment for him was "little faggie boy," and I was right there with them laughing and making fun. When he was around the building, we would snicker and make snide comments about his makeup, tight pants, and heels. We imitated his mannerisms to entertain ourselves, and while all this way going on, I was going to church on Sundays with my mother, arrogantly thinking I was the perfect and pious good Christian because I allowed him to speak to me.

One day at my office, he blurted out, "You don't like me much do you?

"It's not that I don't like you, it's that you are not doing right with God. Your actions are corrupt," I pronounced with great conviction.

"Oh, come on!"

"Really Terry, you need to stop this lifestyle and be the man God made you and stop playing around. What you are doing is an abomination against God."

"Abomination? Do you even know what that means? Do you think I am who I am because I'm bored?" His voice went up an octave, and you could see he was now angry.

"Look, I don't know, we all like to dress up?" I said, trying to soften the escalating conversation.

"Dress up? You have no clue. Hello! This is not a game. This is who I am. Do you think I chose this life?" You could hear the passion in his voice.

"Well, I think you like being 'different' and you could go back to being 'normal' if you wanted."

"Normal? Get a clue, Miss Smarty Pants. This is normal, and stop being so fucking uptight. Jesus, you are such a tight-ass that you squeak when you walk". With that statement, he was out the door, stomping down the hall in his wooden clogs.

For two weeks I didn't see Terry and was actually relieved because I didn't have to deal with our conversations anymore. I was thinking, good riddance, he was such a drama queen and needed to grow up and stop being a flamer.

It was quiet at seven o'clock in the morning on Friday, as most of the tenants had closed up for the long Memorial Day weekend. I was sitting in Jiyoji drinking my morning coffee and reading the newspaper while George sat behind the counter. As there were no customers, he was already on his second beer of the day.

"Holy shit! What the hell happened to you?" George shouted. I turned around, and there was Terry standing at the entrance to the restaurant in a filthy, torn, bloodied T shirt. His eyes were black and blue, his face was red and puffy, and his lips were cut. Someone had badly beaten him.

George was at his side in an instant and sat him down next to me. Sitting was painful because, we later found out, he had two broken ribs. George disappeared to the back of the restaurant and returned with a half- frozen steak. Ever so gently he placed it on Terry's left eye, which was now almost completely shut.

"I came here because I don't know where to go and I don't want to stay home anymore," he whimpered.

"It's okay, now what happened?" I asked as I got him a cup of coffee.

He began his story. "I was working my usual corner last night and I was gorgeous…new makeup, and my friend, Charity,* had just styled my hair. About one o'clock this morning these two very hand-some marines came by and asked how much I would take for a blow job. I said $20, no discounts, because I'm good. They hemmed and hawed, but finally agreed, and we all jumped into their car and went back to my house."

"The first guy was so fit and good looking I almost didn't want to take his money, but you know, a girl's got to eat. I know he knew I was a male because he was touching and kissing me. I let him touch my privates and that aroused him even more. I could tell he loved what I did for him and he enjoyed our time immensely."

"Well, when I started on the second one, all of a sudden, he starts screaming, 'He's a guy, he's a fucking queer! Joe,* you have just been sucked off by a guy! Get the fuck in here!" And with that he punched me square in my mouth and broke one of my teeth. Blood started pouring from my mouth.

Joe came in and looked at both of us and said, "What! Some fag sucked me? No fucking way!"

"I fell down from the first hit to my face and now both of them jumped on me and were punching and kicking me. What was so wicked was that Joe was hitting and kicking the hardest. I thought he was going to kill me. I fought them off and bit one of Joe's hands as I crawled into my closet and held the door shut. I was screaming at the top of my lungs with blood going down my throat. I was choking, holding on to the door with all my strength. Finally, my neighbors came to my rescue and called the police."

"The police didn't do anything except calm everyone down. They didn't say it was 'assault' because the guys were military, and I can't press charges because I'm only a little faggie boy and a hooker." He looked directly at me as he went on with his story.

I turned beet red as I heard him use my term of endearment for him and looked away.

"As I was talking to the police officer," he continued, "I noticed that the marines had their medical record files in the back seat of their car. Marines always travel with their records and can be court-martialed if they don't. So when the policeman left to talk to them, I grabbed Joe's and took it to my room."

The police told them to leave and as they got into their car, Joe realized his file was missing. He asked the officers if he could talk to me and they agreed.

He came to my door and we faced each other through the screen.

"Can I please have my file back?" he asked.

"I don't have it, sorry."

"Look Ma'am, I need that file. May I please have it back?"

"Don't have it."

'Ma'am, I am sorry about the fight," he said in a soft voice that only he and I could hear. Looking directly into my eyes, he whispered, "Ma'am, I am sorry, about everything." There was sadness in his face now.

"Sorry, I don't have your file, so I guess you will just have to tell your commander how you lost it, won't you?" You will have to explain to him how you were getting your dick sucked off by some guy. What did you say, 'some fag sucked me,' I believe? That should be enough to start a whole new file for you. And maybe you should also tell him and your buddy over there how much you enjoyed it."

"With that, he looked at me and you could see him deflate right then and there. He got in the car and they drove off, all the while Joe was hanging his head."

The steak had now thawed and George removed it from Terry's face.

"You hungry, Princess?" he asked.

"Famished."

"Okay, steak and eggs it is for our Princess," and he threw the steak on the grill. George never was one to worry about food safety or contamination.

"I grill, fry, or boil it, what could go wrong," was his motto.

As George went to get the eggs, I said, "Aren't you afraid they'll come back to your house and hurt you over the records?"

"No, those types don't come back to the scene of the crime. Besides, my roommate is bigger than both of them put together, and now that he knows what happened, he said he'd make sure he's home when I am."

George came back with Terry's steak and eggs but when Terry bit into the steak, he groaned. His mouth was sore and started to bleed again.

"Don't worry Princess, eat the eggs and I'll make the steak into a soup so you can eat it. We'll get you back dancing in your high heels soon," he said as he sat down and opened his third beer.

As Terry started to eat the eggs, he stopped and looked at George and me and started crying again.

"I thought he liked me. Shit, what was I thinking! I'm such a freak! No one could ever like me, much less love me! God hates people like me!"

George and I looked at him and then at each other, and in that moment, my heart broke and my soul was truly moved.

We sat in silence for a few minutes, Terry eating, George drinking, and me sipping my coffee. Finally I said, "Terry, God loves everyone and please forgive me for being so disrespectful to you. I don't know a lot of things, especially when it's about people like you, you know, with your proclivity, but I do know this much…and I know George will agree with me… with your heart of gold, your love of life, and your kindness to everyone, no matter how they treat you, you are by far the most beautiful man in the world".

"You think so?" he said, tears welling in his eyes.

"I know so." I said, with tears now in my eyes.

George looked at us and said, "Well, wait a minute, I don't know about the most beautiful, there's still Sean Connery, Gregory Peck, and George Hamilton, but I'm damn sure with all that makeup on that mug of yours, you are the prettiest guy around here."

We all looked at each other and started laughing, and from that day on, Terry became one of my dearest friends.

I took an interest in his modeling and often came down to see him at Summer Breeze, strutting his booty in gowns and boas. I applauded him when he won a beauty and talent contest at the Glades, one of the first gay bars in Honolulu.

Many times we would sit and drink coffee with George, and as the two of them told their 'war' stories about life, I'd be the judge, deciding which was the best or who was telling a taller tale.

Terry showed me how to be more lady-like, and became my personal life coach before they were in vogue.

"When walking in heels, toes first, ladies do not walk heels first," he told me constantly.

He showed me how to do a better job with my makeup.

"Lipstick can be used for rouge right under the cheekbones when you're in a pinch," or "not too much eye shadow, it makes you look like a hooker and I know about that one, Honey." Best of all, he taught me color coordination. "Sweetheart, yellow and brown are not your colors, and I don't care what your mother says. Blue, green, or red, and for God's sakes, no plaids with stripes. Honestly, what were you thinking?"

Most of all, he taught me more self-confidence, as to who I was as a woman, and to enjoy life a bit more.

Terry is still alive and feisty. He has had his struggles and triumphs, but has always remained positive about living and human kindness. We see each other on occasion for lunch and he continues to amaze me with his stories of life, survival, and of course, love. He changed my life that day long ago and I am a much better person because of him.

I am still a person of faith and an Orthodox Christian, but I don't attend church much these days, since my Mom's passing. I still recite the Angelus on occasion, and one of the most important things to me is that I am no longer a black and white person, but a very gray individual in my thinking.

I realize it takes all kinds of people to raise a world. It was another lesson I learned; always keep an open mind about people, no matter what they look like, or what you imagine they represent, because more often than not, you'll be surprised how much you'll learn if you just give the person a chance to show you.

And as for Terry, in my heart he will forever be the most beautiful man in the world.

CHAPTER SEVENTEEN

I Am Going To Be A Developer Of Real Estate!

Life at the Merchandise Mart was good and I blossomed in my job as a leasing agent and property manager. I had become so good at leasing offices and keeping within budget that I started asking for more to do around the company.

Henry decided to give me some other opportunities. The first assignment was to deliver four subpoenas for demand of back rent from non-paying tenants. I had two days to find them. The first two were easy, I found them in town at their offices. I walked right in and asked for Mr. So-and-so, saying I was from the newspaper and wanted to interview him about his new award.

A new award? No one knew about it, but sure enough, the thought of an award was sufficient to flush him out. Most people, whether they like to admit it or not, have egos the size of the state of

Texas. So when he walked into the reception area, I handed him the document, and said "Have a good day!" and left before he knew what had happened. The second one was very much the same, and I began to think this was a simple assignment.

However, the other two were far more difficult. One was a young artist who stopped paying rent on her studio. She was living in a shack just below the Boys Scout camp in Pupukea on the North Shore. I had to hike in and when she saw me, she immediately knew why I had come. With a baby on one hip, and a toddler holding her other hand, I knew money was a big issue for she and her husband. They were both younger than I, hippies from the mainland. He was trying to farm a portion of their rented plot, but with constant rain that year, things were pretty meager and you could see they were hungry.

"I have no money, but will you take a painting I just finished as payment?" she quietly asked. It was an airbrush of the waves at Sunset Beach, about four feet by three feet. It was beautiful and I could see she had a great deal of talent.

"I can't promise you anything." I said.

In the end, I took the painting and told Henry and the owner of the building that dragging her into court was a waste of money and they agreed to write off the lost rent. The painting went to the owner who hated it, but the last time I was in his office, it was hanging in his reception room like an old trophy.

The last assignment was the most difficult as he was an old tenant, Stewart McQueen* who had several shops throughout Honolulu and often refused to pay his rent for months until concessions were granted by his landlords. His staff knew the drill and hid him from anyone who wanted to serve papers on him.

It was now two o'clock and I had until four to get to him. I waited around his office thinking he would eventually emerge. As it got later and there was no sign of him, an idea hit me as I thought of Robert Maccie and his wife. I called his office and said ever so sweetly to his secretary,

"Hello, I'm Stephany, Mr. McQueen's college roommate's daughter. I'm only here for a day before I leave for Maui and Dad wanted me to give Mr. McQueen his birthday present."

"Oh, how sweet, but he is at a doctor's appointment and won't be back today."

"Doctor's appointment? I hope it's nothing serious?" I said showing concern.

"No just Dr. Nakamura,* his dermatologist." she said.

"Okay, well maybe I'll just drop it off at your office later."

I quickly looked up Dr. Nakamura's address in the telephone book and got there just as Mr. McQueen stepped into the reception area. I handed him the subpoena and his mouth was still open as I turned and left the room.

When I got back to the office at three minutes after four o'clock, Henry, Allan, Gwendolyn, and the secretaries all started clapping and saying "Well done!" Mr. McQueen had called Henry from Dr. Nakamura's office fuming and said a check would be coming next week.

About this time I started to do a great deal of the leasing on behalf of the company for most of the buildings it managed. Within the year, everyone was calling me the "Leasing Queen," as I had released ninety of the one hundred fifteen spaces at the Merchandise Mart, and fifteen spaces at other buildings. I even leased an office to Tommy Sands, one of America's teen idols of the 1950's and 1960's, along with Fabian, Frankie Avalon, and Annette Funicello. When I brought him into the office to sign his lease, Gwendolyn, the stoic, always the straight-laced professional, actually blushed when I introduced them and giggled when she shook his hand.

However, all this additional work for the company and its clients did not bring any more money to me. During my first year, I received a $50 monthly raise which brought my salary to $900, a five percent increase. Although I wanted more, I understood it was good compensation, percentage-wise. After my second year, however, with all the increased rental income I had obtained for the company, as well as the commissions I saved them, I was surprised when I only received another $50 a month increase. When I asked Henry, he seemed surprised and a bit annoyed.

"A five percent raise is a lot of money. The accountants are only averaging three percent raises this year," he said.

"But I saved the company $10,000 this year in commissions and increased income for the owners by $4,500 per month," I said.

The secretaries had helped me keep a log of the income and savings on transactions so I would be prepared for Henry. If you wanted something from him, you had to justify it with data or he would immediately deny it.

"That is your job. You're supposed to do that, and I had to jump through a lot of hoops to get you that much because some people didn't think you deserved it."

Allan's name came immediately to my mind. Our conversation ended, and as I walked out of his office, I was now thinking it was time to move on to my next job.

The following Sunday, as fate would have it, I opened the classifieds, and there in the jobs section was a large advertisement… "KACOR Realty, Inc, is looking for a Manager of Marketing and Customer Relations."

One-hundred-fourteen people applied for the position, and only five were selected for interviews. I was interviewed three times, and after calling everyday, twice a day, sometimes even three times for three weeks, I made the cut and was hired. I never really found out if it was my skills or my determined persistence that won me the job.

I walked into Henry's office and announced to him, "I'm going to be a developer of real estate! I just got hired by KACOR Realty; they're the master-plan developers of Hawaii Kai," and with that, I handed him my two-weeks notice.

I could tell from his facial impression that Henry was not pleased with the news. I imagined he was thinking, since he received a bonus from our performance, "There goes one of my meal tickets." But he quickly composed himself and congratulated me. He got up and told Gwendolyn to round up the other property supervisors and managers and together we all went downstairs to Dickens Pub for beers and *pupu*.

CHAPTER EIGHTEEN

Kacor Realty

Henry J. Kaiser was born in Sprout Brook, New York, in 1882 and grew up in poverty. At the age of thirteen, he borrowed five dollars from his sisters and left his childhood home to seek his fortune. That was the end of his formal schooling.

Whatever the disadvantages of his early years, Henry J. Kaiser became one of the greatest industrialists in the world, the father of modern American shipbuilding, and a real estate mogul until his death at age 85 in 1967. His personal philosophy was, "Find a need, and fill it."

During his long and active career, he created Kaiser Aluminum, Kaiser Cement, and Kaiser Steel. At any given time, he had over 40,000 employees working for him.

His companies built the Hoover, Bonneville and Grand Coulee Dams, and over 2,500 Liberty ships for the U.S. Navy during World War II. After the war, the Navy sold 525 of these ships to Greek and

Italian entrepreneurs like Aristotle Onassis, Stavros Niarchos, George Livanos, and Achille Lauro. These ships, which lasted for another twenty-five to thirty years on average, were the basis of their shipping empires.

Mr. Kaiser also created the Henry J. Kaiser Foundation, originally to provide health care for his employees. This program became what is now known as Kaiser Permanente with 167,000 employees who care for 8.7 million health plan members; it was the first health maintenance organization (HMO) in the world and is the prototype of all those in existence today.

Henry Kaiser was said to have built the Kaiser Hawaiian Village Hotel in 1955 (now the Hilton Hawaiian Village) because he was upset that he couldn't find a decent hotel room when he came to Hawaii on vacation. In 1956, Mr. Kaiser wooed Hollywood so he could showcase his new geodesic dome and hotel. He got Michael Todd, Producer of the movie, "Around the World in 80 Days," to hold the premier at the dome. It was quite a success and won best picture at the Oscars' later that year. However, for all who came to the showing that night, their eyes were on Mr. Todd's beautiful, young girl friend and soon-to-be wife, Elizabeth Taylor. From 1955 to 1958, Mr. Kaiser established KHVH radio and KHVH television, which is now KITV4 here in Hawaii.

In 1958, planning to retire permanently in Honolulu, Mr. Kaiser negotiated with Bishop Estate (now known as Kamehameha Schools) for a seven-acre oceanfront, leasehold property at the end of Portlock Road in East Honolulu.

Although Bishop Estate was, and still is, the largest private landowner in the State of Hawaii, it was not actively engaged in developing land. The Trustees had chosen instead to lease their land for long periods of time, rather than to sell it.

Mr. Kaiser built his home, which became known as the Kaiser Estate, and it was unique in that most of the structures were painted in shades of pink, which was his wife, Bess,' favorite color. It also had its own 1,500 square-foot, centrally air-conditioned doghouse and full time dog trainer to take care of their ten poodles. Mr. Kaiser and his staff drove all over Honolulu in pink Jeeps because he had owned the auto company and enjoyed the open-air feel of the car.

In 1961, Trustees of Bishop Estate approached Henry Kaiser and asked if he would be interested in an exclusive agreement to develop 6,000 acres of land from the coastline to the mountains of East Oahu. This section of Honolulu included the areas of Portlock, Hahaione, Kamiloiki, Kaalakei, Kamilonui, Mariners Ridge, Kamehame Ridge, and Kalama Valley.

He was definitely interested, as retirement bored him. An agreement was forged, and that year Kaiser-Aetna became the master-developer of Hawaii Kai, which was centered around the ancient Maunalua fishpond and wetlands known as Kuapa Pond.

Mr. Kaiser, who built his Liberty Ships on an average of four days each, and his geodesic dome at the Hawaiian Village Hotel in twenty hours, was a prolific developer. He believed in planning, then moving full speed ahead. When something needed to get done, it was done, regardless of time or money. Conservation and environmental concerns were not issues in those days.

The Hawaii Kai Master Plan, completed in 1961, was strictly adhered to. Mr. Kaiser was all business, and his drive and determination were instilled in every member of his staff.

By the time Mr. Kaiser died in August 1967, Kuapa Pond had been dredged, and widened, and Hawaii Kai offered housing choices in price, style, view, and location for the more affluent of residents of Hawaii.

However, not everyone was happy with the legacy of Mr. Kaiser and two very volatile incidents arose from his development of East Oahu. These situations were to forever change the lives of many of Hawaii's people, particularly its native Hawaiian citizens, and the very future of the islands. The first was Kalama Valley; the second was the Hawaii Land Reform Act of 1967.

KALAMA VALLEY

World War II brought many people to Hawaii, mostly to the Island of Oahu. When the war ended, military operations rapidly expanded and both the Army and Navy were hungry for housing; when statehood was granted in 1959, development exploded.

The fertile agricultural lands of Oahu were now being bulldozed daily for tract housing, and the rural lifestyle of small family farmers was being wiped out. By the late 1960s, leases in Kalama Valley, where 150 families lived on 250 acres, were on a month-to-month basis. As the housing fury hit peak levels, and the agreement between Kaiser-Aetna (which by then was known as Hawaii Kai Development Corporation, and later as KACOR Realty, Inc.,) and Bishop Estate was in effect, all leases in the valley were terminated to make ready for Kaiser's new subdivision of luxury homes, to be called Craterview. Plans for the project had been submitted to the City and County of Honolulu and adopted by the City Council without change. The plans called for development of single-family subdivisions, a golf course, low-rise apartment units, and a hotel with a restaurant overlooking Makapuu Point in the Queen's Beach area, adjacent to Sandy Beach.

By 1970, only a handful of tenants remained in Kalama Valley and one adamantly refused to leave his home. His name was George

Santos. Mr. Santos, then in his early 60's, had been a pig farmer all his life, like his father and grandfather before him. As long-time tenants of Bishop Estate, the Santos family had raised pigs in Kahala, Hawaii Kai, and Kalama Valley, being forced to leave each site as the land was developed.

Santos said he had had enough and was angry about being "pushed around," and because of his resentment, he did something extraordinary. He went public; he told everyone who would listen that the land was being taken for subdivision and resort use, but that agricultural land and its way of life needed to be preserved. All segments of the media…radio, television, and newspapers, carried his story. At a gathering at the University of Hawaii in October, 1970, he again warned of the major problems facing local people which would devour Hawaii by 1980 if something wasn't done. The first was a wave of big mainland developers, who Santos referred to as "rich guys," coming from the mainland and scooping up all the land; second was the loss of agricultural lands to expensive subdivisions, which would destroy Hawaii as we knew it.

The Chairman of Bishop Estate, Richard Lyman, scoffed at these statements, and even called Kalama Valley, with its former small farms, a "rural slum."

But others listened, especially native Hawaiians, and the students who were beginning to feel the strain of not being able to afford to live in the place they called home. A week and a half after Mr. Santos' visit to the University, over five hundred people met at the State Capitol to protest the expulsion of the Kalama Valley tenants. The rally was sponsored by various churches.

Public support continued to grow, and momentum began to build in protest of the development of Kalama Valley. Many young Hawaiians publicly questioned the Estate's position on agriculture and urbanization, the changing lifestyle. Everyone was debating "quality of life" in discussions in the newspapers, on television, and radio. Young people began to come into the Valley and occupy the now abandoned homes.

A few tenants, including Santos and his 200 pigs, remained at their farms, hoping a compromise would be reached, but by April, 1971, the Estate and Hawaii Kai Development Corporation moved to evict him and the others. Bulldozers were called in and demolition of the homes began.

Throughout the month of April, more and more students came into the valley, and media attention grew intense with the impending evictions. At one point, over three hundred supporters dug in for a war.

On May 11, 1971, everything came to a head when, in a massive demonstration of force, the Honolulu Police Department came into the valley and physically carried out three-dozen non-violent protesters and arrested them for trespassing on Bishop Estate's private property. As the protestors watched from their paddy wagons, the bulldozers moved in and leveled everything.

George Santos was escorted off his property without violence, and his pigs, courtesy of the Estate, were moved two days later to the west side of the Island to a new Waimano piggery. Unfortunately, many of the pigs died from the stress of relocation.

As he was leaving his home for the last time, with TV cameras and newspaper reporters recording events for history, both George and Sam Lono, a *kahuna* and Hawaiian spiritual leader, cursed the land. Broken, and embittered, Santos died within two years of his forced move.

From feelings of despair, a sense of consciousness emerged during those days of dissent for many young native Hawaiians. The injustices they felt from displacement in their homeland formed the beginning of what is now called the "Hawaiian Movement." This movement was to go forward and successfully push for native Hawaiian rights, create the Office of Hawaiian Affairs, defeat the corrupt Bishop Estate Board of Trustees of the 1990's, stop the destruction of the island of Kahoolawe, and get a president of the United States of America to apologize for the illegal overthrow of the Hawaiian monarchy.

After Mr. Santos and the other tenants' departure from the valley, Hawaii Kai Development Corporation moved in and quickly started building homes; sales had already begun and delivery deadlines were looming.

The Craterview houses, designed with high ceilings, spacious living areas, and large bedrooms, averaged 2,250 square feet of interior space. To many local people, this was almost mansion-size as the typical post-war tract house in Hawaii was about 1,100 square feet. Also back then, most houses in Hawaii were built on post and pier, or above ground, for cheaper and easier access to plumbing and electrical connections, The Craterview homes were a combination of stucco and wood built on concrete slabs laid directly on the ground. All of these upgrades were expensive and the homes were considered luxurious; only the wealthier residents of Hawaii could afford them.

Regrettably, in its haste to build these homes, a decision was made to leave the top level of soil on the lots. What no one realized at the time was that Kalama Valley consisted of expansive adobe clay. This dirt contracts in cooler ground temperatures and expands in summer heat.

Within a year, all of the 150 houses started to crack and separate from their foundations. Some walls had cracks as wide as three inches, and garage doors would not shut because the floors were badly slanted.

With lawsuits flying, Hawaii Kai Development honored its responsibilities and repaired every home over the next ten years. One house was so bad it had to be rebuilt from the studs up. What was supposed to have made a large profit, ended up causing the company several millions of dollars due to extensive repairs.

Today the valley has nearly 1,100 homes, and shifting land is still a problem. The soil continues to challenge engineers and builders who are unable to figure out how to stabilize it.

Regardless of scientific explanations, some people familiar with Kalama Valley's history believe it is not the soil that caused the problems, but is in fact, the curse placed on it by Sam Lono and George Santos.

THE HAWAII LAND REFORM ACT OF 1967

In ancient times, the Islands had a feudal land system under which the ruling chief of each island controlled all the land. After Kamehameha I conquered the islands (with the exception of Kauai and Niihau) in 1795, he and his heirs became supreme rulers until The Great Mahele (Land division) of 1848, when, under Kamehameha III, the land was divided with the king retaining his private lands. The remainder of the land was divided between the government, chiefs, and commoners, with approximately one-third going to each.

The king's private lands and those of other high-ranking chiefs, were passed on and eventually inherited by Bernice Pauahi, granddaughter of Kamehameha I, and considered the last of the Kamehameha dynasty. Pauahi married a mainlander, Charles Reed Bishop, founder of Bishop Bank. (Today known as First Hawaiian Bank.) Childless, Pauahi left much of her vast estate for the erection and maintenance of schools for indigent children of Hawaii. Today the

Kamehameha Schools are among the wealthiest private schools in the country.

After annexation in 1898, the Republic of Hawaii ceded to the United States all government lands, giving it ownership of 49 percent of all land in the islands. Forty-seven percent was owned by 72 private landowners, including the largest, Bishop Estate. Only the remaining 4 percent was owned by private individuals or entities.

Statehood, which was granted in 1959, transferred some lands from the federal government to the state. However, it was not until 1967, when the Hawaii State Legislature, believing this tight control of land was oppressive, passed the Hawaii Land Reform Act, which forced private landowners to break up their holdings. Contested, the law made its way to the U. S. Supreme Court where it was upheld.

The state government now had the authority to condemn privately- owned residential land, and made it possible for lessees to buy the fee interest in the land under their homes. Legislators believed this new law would reduce home prices and make housing costs more affordable for local people. In fact, about 15,000 families were able to buy the land under their single-family homes within the first few years of its existence.

The law also weakened control over lands held by the state's large landowners, including Bishop Estate, Damon Estate, and the Estate of James Campbell.

By the time I arrived at KACOR Realty, Inc., in the summer of 1979, its once amicable relationship with Bishop Estate was now somewhat adversarial. As all developers understood, fee simple homes were much easier to sell and they, like others, had heavily supported the Land Reform Act.

Regardless of all the political maneuverings going on, business was booming. The 1970s were great years for KACOR. Projects like Maui Vista and Crestview I and II in Kalama Valley were nearly finished and already sold out. New residential projects, like Marina West, and commercial projects like Hawaii Kai Towne Centre, were in the planning stages with the infrastructure being installed.

It was an exhilarating time to be in development, and the fact that I was now earning double of what I made at the Merchandise Mart thrilled me no end. I had a job in corporate America with great benefits...I could buy a new car, save for a house in Hawaii Kai, and had the boyfriend of my dreams. Life was wonderful, and I envisioned setting the world of real estate development on fire. Or so I thought.

CHAPTER NINETEEN

You're Just Too Aggressive!

I was so excited to finally be working for a big corporation… the master developer of Hawaii Kai! I was going to be part of a team that was creating a new city in Hawaii. However, what I thought would be the ultimate experience of working with one of the greatest companies in America, instead turned out to be one of the biggest nightmares of my career.

KACOR Realty, Inc., formally known as Kaiser-Aetna, Hawaii Kai Development Corporation, and Kaiser Development Company, Inc., was now a wholly owned subsidiary of Kaiser Aluminum and Chemical Corporation. With the name changes came changes to the corporate profile, which promoted the theme of "working together to build a better world." Mr. Kaiser's motto of "Find a need and fix it" was changed to "One person can make a difference."

The headquarters for KACOR were located at 7120 Kalanianaole Highway, which today is the home of 24 Fitness in Hawaii Kai. Built in 1968, it is a 12,000 square-foot, two-story, solid concrete structure adjacent to the marina created from the ancient Kuapa Pond.

KACOR's operating structure was set up so the pecking order and hierarchical command were clearly understood and adhered to at all times. The upstairs housed the president, executive vice presidents, controller, legal department, residential, and commercial project managers, as well as their secretaries. Downstairs were the accountants, engineers, golf course managers, escrow, marketing, and customer relations employees.

You were immediately made aware of your status at the time you were hired. It was explained in detail that your job was either part of "operations" or "staff." Upstairs was for operations, which fed the company and built the profits; downstairs was for staff, which assisted operations in making this profit. When someone was promoted, they, in effect, were literally elevated to top banana status and moved up to the second floor.

The upstairs was very spacious with a large open area separating the legal department and project managers from the executives. The president's office was at the farthest end of the building and every window had a view overlooking the marina. It was spacious, about 1,000 square feet, with its own private conference room. The executive offices were larger then any of the offices downstairs, and all fronted the marina. The secretaries sat outside their bosses' offices. I often thought this arrangement was like guard dogs protecting their masters' houses because you were never allowed to walk into an executive's office without first checking with his secretary. There was a very large conference room at the other end of the floor that could sit twenty people easily, with table and chairs overlooking the Koko Marina Shopping Center and parking lot.

In contrast, the offices downstairs were cramped, and many of the accountants were confined to small workstations. The engineers sat in their minuscule, closed offices which were only big enough for a chair and desk. The marketing and customer relations department shared space with the golf course and marina managers, and sewer facilities department.

The executives took very good care of their employees. The pay scale was top of the market, and raises came often; medical and dental insurance was the best money could buy. The pension plan was one of the finest in the country. You could use the swimming and tennis club free of charge, and fees for a round of golf were either waived or heavily discounted at the two company-owned courses. You were even permitted, when a driver was available, to use the marina boats for personal activities like birthday or graduation parties. When you had been with the company for a few years, you were allowed to purchase a new house in one of the developing subdivisions without closing costs, commission, or fees.

Almost the entire workforce lived in Hawaii Kai; their children went to school together, and everyone knew each other's families. Nepotism was not unusual, but more of a standard. For instance: two of the executive secretaries were sisters; two of the accountants were cousins, and one of the engineers had a son working at one of the golf courses. A younger brother replaced his older brother as one of the in-house attorneys, and the president's nephew had just been hired as a construction cost analyst during my first week on the job.

The corporation provided a lifestyle that many there would never have been able to achieve elsewhere, as well as a comfortable road to retirement. All these perks bred unwavering loyalty. For the employees, their jobs were their lives, and they ferociously protected them. They immediately distrusted unfamiliar people, and God help anyone who was an "outsider." This was the environment I walked into in the summer of 1979.

I was one of the first female mid-level managers with staff under her supervision ever to be hired by KACOR…and I was a complete stranger to them. I was in my mid-twenties, single, lived in Waikiki, and wore slacks instead of suits or dresses. They all knew this about me before I started and the deck was already stacked against me.

It started on my first day, the moment I walked into the building. The receptionist had met me before and knew I was expected, but that didn't matter. I arrived at 8 a. m. sharp and was coldly, but politely, told to take a seat in the lobby. She went about her business, and finally, after making me sit for twenty-five minutes, phoned my boss' secretary to tell her I was in the lobby. She was there in an instant and escorted me upstairs to his office.

After pleasantries, he took me downstairs to my new office and staff. However, it turned out that there was no office for me. The company had been expanding with new personnel. With the newly-hired president's nephew, and a new assistant project manager, there was no more room downstairs. After a few awkward minutes, someone found a cubicle which was being used for storage and faced the parking lot. The cubicle had a World War II type metal desk, a broken chair, and stacks of papers and files. This was where I remained for the next three and half years.

As soon as my boss left, everyone said they had deadlines and couldn't help me organize the office, so for the next two days, I was left to clean it up myself. Both the nephew and I needed new chairs so I asked the customer relations' assistant how to go about getting some. I was told a requisition form would be needed from my boss. It took six months for my chair to arrive, but in a week, the nephew had his.

My staff was composed of six; the marketing coordinator, escrow assistant, her secretary, the customer relations coordinator, the on-staff carpenter, and the department's secretary. They had all been there for years and were very suspicious of me. At least they were courteous; the engineers and accountants despised me on sight, and made no attempt to be pleasant at all. This was the attitude for all my days there; I would forever remain an outsider.

From the time I started, no one downstairs spoke to me, except to say "Hello," with the exception of the nephew, a hard working, straightforward soul. You would have thought nepotism would be bad in this tight-knit company, but in fact, from my observations, all of the relatives proved to be the hardest working employees there. I believe they all thought they had to prove to everyone around that they were worthy.

It was three months before my escrow assistant allowed me time to meet with her, and I was her supervisor. My boss told me to let her come to me and not to bother her unless it was an emergency. As I sat in her spacious office going over various procedures, and forms, she put her right hand in front of my face, stopped me cold with a wave, and in her condescending manner said,

"Look sweetie, I'm not interested in anything you have to say. I have escrows to close and I don't have time for you. You do whatever you do around here and don't bother me and we'll stay friends. If you want something, speak to Elaine,* (her secretary) or the project managers, but don't come into my office again. Now please leave."

With that, she turned her back to me and began to dial her phone. As I walked out humiliated, everyone stood still; they had heard everything because of the openness of the cubicles.

When I later complained to my boss about my treatment, he said, "Well, Miranda* closes all our sales on time and we owe her a lot.

So if I were you, I would cater to her a bit so it doesn't effect your job future here."

Translation: she was more important then I, and I needed to get in line. It was also apparent over the next several months that even though I was responsible for the department, everyone under me was doing their own thing and reporting directly to the project managers without my authorization. The project managers preferred it this way, rather than following the formal policy of going through me.

In addition, the project managers, executive secretaries, and executives enjoyed their petty games, and all took it upon themselves to constantly micro-manage me.

There was an in-house policy that every piece of paper, from legal documentation to Christmas cards, had to have the blessing of everyone before it was sent out. A typical example was: when I wrote a letter to a vendor on KACOR stationary asking for a catalog, the draft letter first went to a project manager, who then sent it to the residential development head, who then sent it to the executive vice president, who then sent it to the legal department, who finally sent it back to me. Everyone always added comments and corrections.

"We don't use 'Aloha', we use 'Very Truly Yours,' more professional," or "please use 'then' not 'than,' that spelling is incorrect, as one project manager said to me on more then one occasion. I would make the requested changes and send it back to the project manager who would then send it back to legal for the final approval. Sometimes, legal would change the letter back to the way I had it the first time, and the whole process would begin again because the project manager didn't like the original wording and this would create inter-office bickering between the legal department and the manager.

A simple letter would take a minimum of a week to be approved and sent out, sometimes two weeks, if the legal department was busy Meanwhile, I sat in limbo, totally frustrated.

Often, the junior attorney called me on the phone to come to his office, and when I arrived, he berated me in front of his secretary or anyone within ten feet of us. Our "discussions," as he defined them, were about me talking to a real estate agent or someone without first getting his approval…or my conversations with my own department, or my letters… anything and everything about what I was doing wrong. When I arrived at his office, his chairs would conveniently have files on them and he made no gesture to remove them, so I had to remain standing.

"I don't think I need your permission to talk to people." I once said.

"You do need my permission on how you present the KACOR image in all things. You do understand to whom you are speaking? I am part of legal and everything goes through us," he began and then on and on he went for another five minutes. He so enjoyed belittling me during our little "chats," that I came to immensely dislike him.

The executive secretaries also delighted in exerting their power over me. They watched and often questioned me about where I was going, why I was going, and with whom was I meeting. They reported to their bosses, who then talked to my boss and the project managers about who I talked to if they saw me outside during lunch or after hours. The president's secretary often called and dictated to me on certain minor items concerning the real estate agents we were working with, and I would have to report to her directly, making sure the project managers and my boss knew what she wanted that week. If I failed to report to her in a timely manner, I was called in by my boss and questioned as to why I did not respond to her fast enough.

It was an unofficial policy that female personnel would wear Hawaiian dresses or *mu'umu'u* on Fridays, and when I didn't, the project managers and executive secretaries politely chided me time and time again. I hated *mu'umu'u* in those days and refused to wear them. I don't doubt this lack of respect for the *mu'umu'u* policy was probably a huge black mark against me.

As marketing manager, I was supposed to come up with creative ideas for marketing our projects, but I was never given the chance. Looking back, I believe the project managers probably didn't want to go through the process with the legal department and have to deal with the attorneys' quirks, so they stayed with what they knew worked, rather than try to reinvent the wheel.

For the most part, I tended to the needs and whims of the haughty real estate agents who were selling our projects. My division provided the information and promotional materials and assisted with their open houses. A sizeable portion of my time was spent acting as the agents' minion for the smallest of issues, and many of them enjoyed bossing me around.

If I complained about my treatment, the project managers would criticize my attitude.

"You need to remember, Stephany, we have an excellent relationship with our "friends" and they pay your salary. If I were you, I would cater to them anytime they're around. They were with us long before you came, and they know how to sell our projects" said George,* one of the two senior residential project managers.

As the customer relations manager, I also spent a lot of time meeting with Craterview homeowners, walking through their cracked houses, and setting up repair schedules.

However, for most of my tenure at KACOR, I spent my days in meetings or conferences. I called myself, "The Meetings Person." I averaged four hours out of a nine-hour day in meetings. The executives wanted to meet on anything and everything. We once even had a ninety-minute department workforce discussion on the "KACOR Image Program-Graphics Manual." It was a ninety-page manual with illustrations and documentation on how to state, write, or present the "KACOR" name and image.

My all-time favorite meeting was when the entire residential development department had to sit in the large conference room for two hours while one of the executives explained to us how to conduct an information meeting for outside vendors or clients.

He droned on and on, finally saying in conclusion, "Now remember the *pigeon syndrome*. This is when you know you have lost the attention of those in the room because all they are doing is nodding their heads up and down when you look at them, like a pigeon cooing. So you must work to keep their attention with jokes or what-have-you."

As I looked around the table, I started to chuckle. The vice president was totally oblivious to his surroundings, and everyone was smiling and nodding their heads.

Many of the conferences were held before 8 am, at lunch time, or after 5 p. m. and often the late gatherings went well past 6 p.m. I started to think the executives hated going home at night and would have these appointments as excuses to miss dinner with their families. I never knew for sure, but it was probably true, at least for some. More importantly, I believe it was a method for management to keep employees in place. To this day, I think the whole process of meetings is often about useless posturing, and for the most part, I loathe them.

Within two weeks after the pigeon syndrome meeting, John,* the other senior residential project manager, took me out to lunch at the shopping center's Mexican restaurant. The ambience was dark and dirty, but the food was excellent. He was an intense, trim man in his middle 30s who had worked his way up the KACOR ladder. We made small talk and when his enchiladas arrived, he ordered additional jalapenos peppers, which he mixed with both the red and green chili sauces. After the first two bites, sweat was pouring off his face.

"I love hot food!" he gasped. I could see his intensity went all the way to his stomach.

"I see that, as opposed to me. I like everything mild and cool after five years of braces. Too hot or too cold... it gives me pain," I said.

John stopped eating, put his fork down and wiped his face. He folded his hands on the table. Looking me squarely in my eyes, he said, "See, that's your problem Stephany. Everything's got to be your way. You need to compromise and work with the team more."

"Oh, please, give me a fricking break! I'm everyone's lackey as it is now. I get all the crappy jobs, like kissing the butts of dumber than dumb real estate agents. Do you know, the other day one called me and asked why the brochures say *marketing* and not *selling* of Hawaii Kai and I had to bite my tongue. Or sitting there getting my butt chewed out because homeowners are pissed off that their houses are falling down in Kalama Valley. I do a lot for the team as it is!" I said.

"I'm telling you, as someone who actually likes working with you, you need to tone down. You're just too aggressive. People are very uncomfortable around you."

"I'm not aggressive. I'm assertive. There's a difference. An aggressive person will push for his or her ideas and step on people to get what they want. An assertive person is concerned about other people's feelings and is considerate of them when trying to achieve goals.

I've always been polite and considerate to everyone in the company," I said as I stabbed into my tacos.

"And, that's another thing. What is the deal with everyone telling me what to do? No one is ever concerned about my feelings. I feel like a tennis ball being batted back and forth for everyone's entertainment."

He ignored this part of my comment and continued, "People around here believe aggressive and assertive are one and the same and you need to tone it down a notch."

"John, just because I look someone in the eye and tell them what I'm thinking shouldn't be a negative. Sometimes it's good to have contrary ideas. I've always thought people should be upfront and know where they stand. That's a positive in my book."

"People think when you look them directly in the eye, you're challenging them. They don't like you to be so straightforward. They feel you're being confrontational. That is not the way we work here. You need to cut it down and be a team player. Now please pass me the red chili sauce. I do love hot food."

I felt so frustrated. I was once again made aware that nothing I did was correct, but after that lunch, I did start to wear *mu'umu'u* on Fridays. I hoped that would at least show I wanted to be part of the team.

In my third year at KACOR, business slowed way down because of rising interest rates. In the summer of 1981, Paul Volcker, who was the Chairman of the Federal Reserve under President Reagan, needed to kill inflation, which was at the highest since 1946 and had been crippling the country. He did this by slowing down the economy and allowing the primary rate charged to banks from the Reserve to go up to 21.5%. These rates had not been seen since the days of the U.S. Civil War. This meant anyone who needed financing from a bank or savings and loan to purchase property was paying a mortgage interest rate of 22 to 23 percent. By the spring of 1982, KACOR was offering its own agreement of sale financing package at 12 percent per annum.

It became my dubious job to contact these buyers directly and follow up on the scheduled closing for their properties. Some purchasers took the KACOR financing because they had put down their 20 percent cash deposit on the home of their dreams and could not get the money back from the company. The in-house attorneys made sure the contracts were ironclad.

However, for many, the high rates were too much and they walked away from their deposits, which for a lot of them, was their life savings. Within a few months, nothing was closing, construction was halted, and housing inventory was increasing at a rapid pace.

With business turning negative and knowing that the real estate business moves in cycles, the pressure was on to regroup and prepare for the next round of development, especially with politicians.

In the real world of real estate development, developers can't function without certain "friends" behind them. City and state employees, especially city councilmen, or the mayor, need to be on the developer's side to get approval for items like designating roads and sewer lines, zoning changes, and land variances. Without these links to political power, a developer has no chance in Hades of meeting deadlines on financing and sales. Nothing would ever move forward. Many developers buy fundraiser tickets for politicians, and some hire former legislators or councilmen to be their "Vice President of Community Relations," or "Community Liaison Officer" or something to that effect, to lobby for them so they can get their projects completed. This was the way of the land back then, and in my opinion, with the tremendous costs of construction, continues to be so today.

Late one Friday afternoon, George called me into his office. As I sat down, he placed $10,000 worth of fundraiser tickets for a current councilman in front of me.

"I need you to have your vendors, real estate agents, and personal friends buy these tickets for my friend, Councilman Pagoda.* When you sell these, I have another $10,000 more for you to sell."

"But George, I don't solicit vendors, agents, or personal friends. It's something I don't like doing and I believe it affects my creditability particularly with real estate agents."

"Councilman Pagoda has been very helpful and is a personal friend of mine. I need your help on this."

"Look George, this is not in my job description," I retorted with a bit of ire in my voice.

"You need to help me," he continued.

"I'm sorry, but I can't help you with this. He is your buddy and this is something you need to do on your own. I just don't feel comfortable with it."

With that comment, he narrowed his eyes and smiled. I could see that a line had been drawn and I was now the enemy.

A month after George and I met, my boss left for a better paying job with more autonomy and independence. He had been the most kind and thoughtful person I would ever know there. He protected me, and when he left for his new job, I knew my days were numbered, but didn't realize how fast my exodus would be.

Business was now in the toilet with the interest rates skyrocketing and there was no end in sight. Shortly after my boss's departure, a decision was made to reduce personnel and everyone was nervous. They didn't have to worry because I was the first to be cut, along with the assistant golf course manager.

In my meeting with the Executive Vice President, I asked him why I was being laid off when I was senior to five others in the company. We both knew why I was going first, but he looked at me said,

"You're a single woman and those guys are married with wives and children. They need to feed their families. You don't have to worry about those things. Your folks and boyfriend will take care of you. And you can always move out of your apartment and back home with your parents."

"That's not fair, I need money too." I said.

"Life is not always fair," he grinned.

I was given two weeks of severance pay and allowed to collect six months of unemployment. I cleared out my desk and left the office for the last time.

Looking back on my experience at KACOR, what I failed to realize because of my naivety, was that when coming into a tightly controlled environment, a company is only as good as the people in it. In their defense, maybe because of their experiences with Kalama Valley and the Hawaii Land Reform Act of 1967, there was more fear of outsiders than in normal situations.

For me, the bias I experienced determined much of my fate during my tenure in corporate America. It also shaped my unwavering determination to become independent. It was another lesson I learned about business and real estate. Large corporations are often made up of small-minded people.

CHAPTER TWENTY

Kuhio Mall

I drove home, crying all the way, then went to bed for the next three days. Nothing I said or did had been right for over three and a half years; I felt worthless.

After a week of sulking, I emerged from my personal abyss and started the job search process over again. For the next five and a half months, I sent out resume after resume to various companies, 150 in all, but there were no jobs available. Interest rates were hovering between 18 to 22 percent. No one was hiring, especially in real estate.

The level of depression I suffered was something I had never experienced, and it must have shown vividly. At one of my last interviews before my insurance ran out, the employment counselor at the state's unemployment office, a small, frail, local Japanese woman stopped working on her report, looked up at me and said, "I'm so sorry you're going through all this. You have a good background and I know you will find something soon. Something that will raise you to a higher level than you were before."

Her kind words were like a glass of cool water to my dehydrated soul. Even today, when I get down, I still recall her compassion and sympathy.

Finally, with two weeks left of unemployment insurance, my two credit cards almost maxed out, my parents both physically sick and unable to help me, I started to look at any and every job out there. A new determination came into me and I thought to myself, "If I have to clean toilets, so be it. I will be the best damn janitor out there!"

As I was scouring the want ads on a typical Sunday morning, I saw a small, one inch by one inch blind ad which simply stated, "Manager Wanted! Send your resume to post office box ****, Honolulu, HI 96815." It was so small, I missed it the first time I went through the classifieds, but, it caught me the second time around and my resume was in the mail Monday morning. On Wednesday, I received a telephone call to schedule an interview for the coming Friday with the owner of the Coral Reef Hotel. I hadn't thought about the hotel business, but I was willing to try anything.

The owner of the Coral Reef turned out to be Andre Tatibouet. His family owned the Hotel Corporation of the Pacific, or Hotel Corp., as everyone referred to it, which at the time of my interview, managed or owned over twelve condominiums, hotels, and one shopping center in Hawaii. Among them were the Coral Reef, Kuhiolani, Waikikian, Diamond Head Beach Hotel, Waikiki Surfside, Waikiki Sunset, Waikiki Gateway and Kuhio Mall on Oahu; Coco Palms, Kona Islander Inn, Island Colony, and Kaanapali Shores were located on outside islands. To say he was a major player in the local hotel business at the time is an understatement.

Hotel Corp. started as a hotel company in 1948 when Andre's parents built a small, fourteen-room hotel at the corner of Kuhio Avenue and Uluniu Street in Waikiki. The land had been acquired by Andre's mother's family years before through friendships with the royal families of Hawaii. Andre's mother, Annalie Knaack, married Joseph Jean Tatibouet ("Tati"), a handsome Frenchman from Brittany, in 1938. Together they built and ran the tiny hotel called the Royal Grove. Their room rates averaged $5 per night, and Mr. and Mrs. T., as they were called, were the concierge, maids, janitors, and hosts.

Andre grew up in the hotel and was sweeping floors and helping the maids clean rooms at the age of six, learning the business from the ground up. In 1959, when Andre was just eighteen, and a freshman at the University of Hawaii majoring in Russian History, he embarked on his first development with his family's blessing. He built the fourteen-room Cleghorn Apartment Hotel, named for Princess Kaiulani's father, Archibald Cleghorn, which was located across the street from the Royal Grove. After graduation, Andre took over the family business, and in 1968, incorporated the company and became its president, with his mother, Annalie, as Chairman of the Board.

In 1969, Andre built the Pacific Beach Hotel, with its 360 rooms. In 1978, along with Herbert Horita, a successful developer of many residential properties and subdivisions on the west side of Honolulu, they developed the Waikiki Sunset Condominiums and the Kuhio Mall.

The corporate offices of Hotel Corp. were on two floors of the Coral Reef. The executive offices were refurbished hotel rooms…not very opulent, but private and comfortable. Everyone, from secretaries to senior staff, appeared relaxed and comfortable with one another.

Andre warmly greeted me as I walked into his office. He was impeccably dressed in a crisp, pressed, white, long-sleeved shirt, red tie, and highly polished black loafers. He wore heavy gray wool trousers, which I thought odd for Hawaii's 85 degree temperature until I realized he kept the air conditioning at a consistent 65 degrees. He was tall, thin, with reddish brown hair and bright blue eyes. I thought he looked much younger than his forty-two years.

His real estate consultant also welcomed me. Edward* was more casual than Andre, dressed in a subdued aloha shirt with brown slacks and matching brown loafers which complimented his completely white hair and crystal blue eyes. He was very fit for fifty-four, and tanned from kayaking, I later found out. Edward had been a Marine platoon leader in Vietnam and was very amicable, extremely well organized, and a quick study of people.

As I sat down, Andre took a drag off his cigarette, part of his two-to-three pack a day habit, and confided that out of ninety-three applicants, he had chosen me after reviewing my resume, sight unseen, because he knew my brother, Steven, and my mother. That convinced him I would be a good worker. "Well," I thought, "So much for a college education and years of experience, but thank God for my brother and mother to get me off unemployment."

Andre had worked with my brother over the years on various commercial leases, and knew my mother because they had collaborated on setting the groundwork for founding Pacific Preparatory Academy in 1963. Andre, in those days, was much like the school he had brought to fruition; innovative, freethinking, and willing to try new ideas. Status quo had not gotten him where he was in the hotel business.

I was hired as the general manager of Kuhio Mall, with both Andre and Edward as my direct supervisors. My responsibilities included all commercial leasing for the Mall and other hotel properties as needed, and to overseeing the fiscal and operational management of the Mall. My salary was a base with incentives and bonuses if I reached certain goals.

I was to start the next day, and Andre and Edward told me they wanted me to "think outside the box," and to make the Mall a profit center. They promised to support me in everything I did, as long as the owners did not have to make any financial contributions. They were very specific: any renovations, promotions, or advertising had to come directly from the tenants and leasing income.

I immediately loved the fact that I would be working with Andre and Edward. I could see, as my interview continued, they appreciated my intellect and sense of humor, and gave me, within reason, free rein over the Mall.

Kuhio Mall, built in 1978 and known today as the Waikiki Town Centre, is a three-story shopping complex, 74,000 square feet of gross leasable area, the equivalent of nearly two acres of vertical retail space adjacent to the International Marketplace in the heart of Waikiki. When I became its GM, it was bleeding the owners dry by losing over $50,000 per month, which was a lot of money in those days. So much money, in fact, that the banks were threatening to call their loans, and with interest rates still at 18%, restructuring the loans was impossible. It was essential that each property stand on its own and not be used as collateral for more profitable assets, as one bad property could negatively impact the others with cross-financing. Kuhio Mall needed to make more money or go into foreclosure; there was no other option at the time.

The previous manager had tried to separate the mall from its abutting neighbor, International Marketplace, by blocking the adjoining entryways and keeping its concrete walls bare. She wanted the mall to stand alone, as its own destination location. I, on the other hand, saw the need to piggyback off of the most successful retail concept ever created in Waikiki.

The first thing I did was to assemble my team, which consisted of a bookkeeper to oversee the receivables and payables, a personal secretary, a management supervisor and crew, and a security chief with six officers. Then we got the staff on the move and opened up the walkways and decorated them with Polynesian decor so the tourists didn't notice they were flowing from one shopping area to another. We then set out to "green" the Mall by planting vines along the walls. Then the maintenance department built and installed planter boxes everywhere possible and placed hanging baskets along the railings filled with brightly flowering plants. I had all the non-structural walls in the center of the mall removed to allow room for kiosks, as I had observed that tourists enjoyed poking around them, and usually ended up buying several items. My secretary called different shopping centers and schools in the State looking for groups in search of a venue for performing. We got schools choirs, bands, storytellers, aspiring musicians, and others to come to the mall and perform, all for free. We even found a group of singing nuns from Ohio looking for a place to croon for donations. They performed at the mall for three days straight, and both the tenants and tourists loved them.

We even put together a TV ad for the mall, which had never been done for a Waikiki retail property. It starred many of the tenants, Edward, my staff, and me. It's still floating around today when you view "You Tube" and look at the 1980s Hawaii commercials.

Finally, through leasing efforts, I slowly changed some of the kiosk tenants who sold mostly tee shirts and trinkets from China and the Philippines with *Hawaii* printed on them and replaced them with a popcorn maker, hot dog stand, flower seller and lei maker. The income from the mall steadily increased, and within two years, we were able to decrease the bleeding to only $20,000 per month, down from the previous $50,000. Although we were still losing money, Andre and Edward could see light at the end of the tunnel and were very pleased.

I felt I had finally found my niche in the business of shopping center management, particularly in Waikiki. It was exciting and stimulating, with so many different moving parts and people. I felt I was the Master of my own ship, as my Dad would often tell me, and life was good.

CHAPTER TWENTY-ONE

"Sex In The City" – Commerical

Conventions, conventions, conventions! God, how commercial real estate people love them. The bigger the better. Exotic locales? You know it! There are conferences also known as mini-conventions all over the world: London, New York, Milan, Tokyo, New Orleans, Sydney, Athens, Honolulu. But the big annual conventions which everyone salivates over like a new fisherman catching his first big-eyed tuna is, of course, Sin City, or as most people know it, Las Vegas, Nevada. Why? Because for a price, anything and anyone you may ever have desired is available there.

Annual conventions have anywhere from up to 30,000 delegates and there are probably another 60,000+ people who come into town to participate in the production. That's a lot of anonymity for a week. During the days that a convention lasts, there are deal-making sessions, classes, networking meetings, breakfast conferences, and top-notch celebrity luncheon speakers. There are miles and miles of displays, kiosks, and food courts showcasing the wares and products of developers, vendors, banks, leasing agents, and retailers.

At night, however, conventioneers are free and the town is made for play and partying. Most delegates come without their spouses, giving them freedom from the "old ball and chain," an abundance of beautiful people, a 24-hour party zone, and flowing alcohol, all of which make them a lot bolder in seeking what they want, and ultimately will pay for, in the late hours.

Many dress to the nines and strut their stuff because there are the 90,000 plus people all in the same area, bored out of their minds after the third day of working non-stop, just waiting for a chance to say, like the Lady Marmalade song goes, "Voulez-vous coucher avec moi ce soir." And if this isn't the delegates' preference because of too much familiarity within the business environment, then there is always the opportunity to enjoy the company of "escorts." Yes, prostitution is illegal in Clark County, but let's be real…

At a convention I attended in 2010, one of our Hawaii guys whom I know very well decided to pick up a "working girl" outside the Flamingo Hotel. He got liquored up and took her up to his room even after I and a few other Hawaii people said don't do it. He spent the night with her and had a grand time, but when he awoke she was gone, along with his Rolex stainless steel submariner and wedding ring that were laying on the dresser. He didn't report the theft because it would involve a police report and he didn't want his wife to find out. When he got back to Honolulu he told his wife he lost his jewelry when he left them in a rented golf bag. When we met up for breakfast a few days later, I told him in the future if he was going to be stupid and risk his marriage, then to go naked but keep his damn jewelry on at all times. Later that year his wife felt bad for him and purchased a new Citizen's wristwatch and wedding band, which he wears today. When I last saw him a few months ago, he said he still misses his Rolex, but is looking forward to the next convention.

And then there was James Steele.* Jim was one of the top commercial brokers in Hawaii at the time when I attended another one of these conventions. He was a former Marine POW in the Vietnam War and escaped twice, the second time saying he would find a way out or die, but he was never going back to the brutal existence of the prison camp. He found freedom and from that moment on never looked back, believing time was an extra gift and he was going to enjoy himself at every opportunity. He was very good looking and looked like a small bear with horn-rimmed glasses. He had a great self-depreciating sense of humor and was the most affable fellow you would ever want to meet. He always dressed well in highly starched, striped, long-sleeved Polo shirts, wool slacks, and gleaming polished shoes. When I knew him he was on the top of his game and many a commercial agent was jealous of him. Much of his success was from his personality and ability to hold his liquor. He worked for a well-known commercial brokerage house and his main job was to entertain and "soften" the clients up to make the deal. Softening was anything from hopping from one Korean bar to another, dining at La Mer, and playing endless rounds of golf at Waialae Country Club.

Many of us were on the plane with Jim when we landed at McCarran International Airport in Vegas. Within two hours of landing, Jim had picked up two of the most gorgeous, buxom blondes from his favorite escort service. There was one on each of his arms for the entire five days; they stayed in his room, and attended all the functions with him. When chatting with them at one of the cocktail parties for the Hawaii delegation, they were not very cerebral and mainly interested in fashion and jewelry, but they were stunning and all the fellows constantly fluttered about them, offering drinks to get their attention.

Many think that what happens in Vegas, stays in Vegas, and that may be the case for most, but unfortunately for Hawaii delegates, that is not true because the "coconut wireless" is strong in paradise and everyone knows everything about everybody. Before long even the spouses find out and that was the case with Jim. His wife at first didn't leave him because he adorned her with jewelry and spa treatments, but after a time, the marriage amicably ended, as he was a very generous man. Jim moved to the mainland several years ago to pursue larger fish, but I hear from him occasionally. He is now on wife number five, semi-retired, drinks several cocktails a day, and still enjoys attending conventions.

CHAPTER TWENTY-TWO

A Real Estate Diva Is Born

As a senior manager of Hotel Corp.'s employee family, I could travel and stay at any of our resorts for just the cost of the cleaning fee. Many times my boy friend and I would jump on an inter-island plane and fly to Maui where we would meet our friends and spend the weekend playing golf at Kapalua, lunching at the Hyatt Regency, and sipping cocktails while watching the whales at sunset in Lahaina.

I learned how to ski at Lake Tahoe with a group of top executives when we all went to see the Bill Cosby show on a whim over a long weekend. My bonuses gave me extra cash, and I spent a lot of it on memberships at Oahu Country Club, Outrigger Canoe Club, and the Honolulu Club. I even flew in a private plane to Kalaupapa for a personal one-on-one tour of the settlement with Richard Marks, the unofficial mayor of the village and a former Hansen's disease patient, or as he preferred to be called, a former leprosy patient.

Every weekend I attended cocktail parties. One of them was at a plush Kahala home on the beach, which was hosted by an attorney who drove around in his Rolls Royce with license plates that stated, "SUE EM." At the party, Alexandria Czar* one of the most influential marketing people in town because of her connections in Hollywood, showed up dressed in a too-tight-for-her-figure leopard dress. Her husband, in black leather pants, vest, and wearing a rhinestone dog collar attached to the leash she was holding, accompanied her throughout the evening.

Occasionally, when Andre's wife was out of town, he asked me to accompany him to various events to which he had been invited, and I got to meet some of the most amazing people of the times. One was a major real estate developer in Hawaii and his young, stunningly beautiful, South American wife. She was referred to around town as "The Argentina Firecracker" because of her wit and beauty.

Another remarkable personality I met through Andre was Donn the Beachcomber. By the time I met Donn Beach, he was in his mid seventies, with a zest for life unmatched by all. His office was a tree house in the enormous banyan tree in the center of International Marketplace. I often climbed up to see him and we would chat as we watched the tourists strolling by, some thirty feet below.

Donn the Beachcomber was born Ernest Raymond Beaumont Gantt in Texas, and is considered the father of "Tiki" restaurants and bars, along with Victor Jules Bergeron, Jr., or, as everyone called him, Trader Vic. They were amicable competitors and both created the Tiki Bar culture which was popular from the 1930s through the 1970s, with sixteen Don the Beachcombers and twenty-five Trader Vics restaurants, mostly on the West Coast. Both of them claimed to have created the Mai Tai, but I truly believe it was Donn's invention as he was drinking them in the 1930s, long before Trader Vic appeared on the scene in the 1940s.

Donn created sixty-four drink recipes in all, most of them using rum. Among them were the Mai Tai, Zombie, Navy Grog, Missionary's Downfall, Tahitian Rum Punch, Cobra's Fang, Shark's Tooth, Skull and Bones, Test Pilot, Mystery Gardenia, and Never Say Die.

Another special person I met during those years was iconic kumu hula, Faye Pomaialoha Dalire, and her *hula halau*, Keolalaulani Halau Olapa O Laka. They were our Hawaiian entertainers at the Mall, performing six days a week. Each year I attended the Merrie Monarch Festival in Hilo as her guest, and there I met all of the most famous and talented artists and performers of Hawaiian dance and culture. Aloha, as she is known, has the distinct honor of being crowned the first "Miss Aloha Hula" at the festival in 1971, and her three daughters continued the family tradition as each one of them has won the title, carrying on the legacy of their grandmother, Mary Keolalaulani McCabe Wong who started the *halau*.

In this ambiance I became intoxicated with the perks and power of being a player in the Waikiki scene. I was schooled by Andre and Edward, as well as the other executives at Hotel Corp. that landlords on the mainland looked at their tenants as business partners because good tenants were hard to find, but here in Hawaii it was just the opposite, especially in Waikiki. Tourism was exploding, money was flowing, and retailers were hungry for Hawaii locations. During these go-go years, landlords looked at their properties as fiefdoms and their tenants as serfs. This was particularly true if the shop owner was a small local business. The tenant was to serve the master, and if lucky, might even make a profit.

In these surroundings, when you have absolute control, a certain amount of arrogance and conceit sets in, and I was no different. The majority of tenants in Waikiki, including the Mall, were immigrant Koreans and Vietnamese who had come to America for a better way of life. They worked twelve-hour days, seven days a week, often caring for their newborn children parked next to their carts. They had spent their life savings on a shop space. When I walked around the center, they were truly terrified of me because they could lose their life-blood in an instant with the thirty-day cancellation clause I had in all license agreements.

In addition, when residential agents or "amateur negotiators" as I called them, came by trying to do a commercial lease, I showed them no respect as they infuriated me. It was my experience that they desired the commission, but didn't want to take the time to become skilled in all the requirements needed to complete a transaction. They often looked for short cuts to increase their income and this was when mistakes happened. I was brutal to them, and they, like the tenants, were afraid of me. The fear made me feel powerful and I showed no mercy to anyone who didn't do his or her job well, or pay the rent on time. A real estate diva was born, and I ruled with an iron fist.

CHAPTER TWENTY-THREE

Hawaii's Own Bernie Madoff

In 1978, a new investment company was incorporated in Honolulu with Ronald Rewald and Sunlin "Sunny" Wong as co-owners. It was called Bishop Baldwin Rewald Dillingham & Wong. Among the names were those of three old, prominent, Hawaii families which had no connection to the company. The local names came from Charles Reed Bishop, husband of Princess Pauahi and founder of First Hawaiian Bank; Henry Alexander Baldwin, of the publicly traded company of Alexander and Baldwin, and Benjamin Dillingham, founder of Oahu Railway and Land Company, which later became Dillingham Corporation, builder of Ala Moana Shopping Center. Ronald Rewald was chairman of the board and treasurer; Sunny Wong was president and CEO of the company.

There was the well-established rumor around town that Mr. Rewald had played professional football with the Cleveland Browns of the National Football League and the Kansas City Chiefs of the American League in the 1960s, and had parlayed his football money into millions in the stock and real estate markets. When he first arrived in Hawaii, he purchased a multi-million-dollar home on Kalanianaole Hwy with a paddle tennis court that sat on Paiko Lagoon. He was the talk of the town and everyone agreed he had come to Honolulu to take his empire global.

The firm hired the best and brightest attorneys, accountants, and investment brokers that money could buy. After setting up their offices and touting the businesses they owned throughout the world, they proceeded to buy the Hawaii Polo and Racing Club in Moku-leia, and Motorcars of Hawaii, the exclusive auto dealership for exotic cars like Lamborghinis, Roll Royces, Maseratis, and Ferraris.

Bishop Baldwin, as they came to be known, declared in its presentations to clients that up to $150,000 of their money would be protected under the Federal Deposit Insurance Corporation, or FDIC. They also guaranteed returns on their investments of a minimum of 20 percent annually.

The 20 percent return did not appear to be an overstatement because those were the days of the Carter/Reagan administrations when interest rates on home loans were at 22 percent, and certificates of deposit were yielding 18 percent per annum. However, it seemed that no one in Honolulu questioned the use of the famous family names, and more importantly, not a soul noticed an immediate red flag. The company was not a chartered bank and because of this, it was not qualified to have FDIC insurance.

By 1983, over four hundred Hawaii people had invested $22,000,000 in Bishop Baldwin, and the company was flying high.

It had 120 employees, or as they were referred to, "consultants," in sixteen countries, including Hong Kong, China, Singapore, Indonesia, Taiwan, India, New Zealand, Australia, England, France, Sweden, Brazil, and Chile. The headquarters of the company was Honolulu, at Grosvenor Center, which is now the Pacific Guardian Center. It took up three floors of the building and Mr. Rewald's personal office was on the 26th floor and covered over 1,500 square feet, the size of an average house in Hawaii. It was five-sided, with the first three sides constructed of glass with spectacular views of the ocean and Waianae coast. The fourth wall contained his desk area, and the fifth wall had a water feature about ten feet high, with water gently flowing down Hawaiian lava rocks to create a dramatic tropical atmosphere.

The consultants in the company were paid extremely well, with a base salary of about $75,000 to $85,000, with bonuses for bringing new clients to the company. This was amazing pay when you remember the average salary in Honolulu at the time was $25,000 per year.

One of the perks of working for the firm was a membership in the Honolulu Club. The Honolulu Club, which opened in 1980, is still in operation. It is located in an eight story building on the corner of Ward Avenue and King Street where the old Trader Vic's Bar and Restaurant was, and was the first of its kind in Hawaii, before the arrival of Gold's Gym and 24-Hour Fitness. It featured formal dining, a bar looking down on the racquetball courts, state of the art gym facilities, a full size tennis court, squash, paddle tennis and racquetball courts, swimming pool, spa, massage service, 24-hour activities, and easy parking.

I joined the club as one of its first hundred members in 1979 before it was even built because I was living in Makiki just five minutes away and had become bored with the beach scene now that I had "retired" from surfing. Being an avid tennis player since high school, I quickly jumped into racquetball, and even won a couple of "C" Division tournaments.

I loved playing with the guys for the competition, and in 1982 met Sunny Wong. He was handsome, charming, and forever the quintessential gentleman. He seemed to spend a lot of time at the club; you knew he was around if there was a parked Ferrari, Maserati, or Lamborghini outside in the porte-cochere adjacent to the club's entrance. When I was there, we often played a few rounds on the court. He was lean, muscular, and extremely quick. I think he toyed with me when I got a couple of points off of him, and I don't remember that I ever won a game.

Within a few weeks of our getting acquainted, he introduced me to one of his consultants who specialized in real estate. Jack Madison* was originally from Santa Barbara, California, and graduated from the University of Southern California with a degree in Finance. He was blond, blue eyed, six feet two inches tall, beefy, a couple of years younger than I, quite cocky, and we hit it off immediately. He wasn't a very good racquetball player, but he was a practiced drinker from his fraternity days. What made him so enchanting to be with was that he was quite the dancer and I learned how to foxtrot and do a little quickstep, which for me, with my two left feet, was somewhat of an accomplishment.

Jack and I, when we began dating, often met for lunch, and one day we met at his office and he showed me around. Mr. Rewald was out of town and Jack took me to see his office. When I walked in, the size, flowing waterfall, and magnificent views took my breath away. His desk must have been ten feet long and six feet wide, with several sets of telephones sitting on it, and his college degree from Marquette University in Milwaukee, Wisconsin, prominently displayed behind it. There was a formal seating area to the side, quite like the Oval Office.

"Impressive, isn't it?" Jack said.

"Wow, how do you guys afford all this," I said.

"We have clients all over the world, and the money just seems to be pouring in from everywhere. We're looking at everything and buying companies all over the globe."

"Have you done any deals yet?" I asked.

"Well no, not yet, and no one else has in my division, but I think soon."

"But, you aren't licensed here to buy or sell."

"Doesn't matter. When you have the cash, everybody wants you and licenses don't mean anything."

During the next several months that we went out together, Jack often hinted I would make a good candidate for the firm. Sunny then asked me if I would come and work for the company. Both Jack and Sunny thought I could help in their future plans for real estate acquisitions in Hawaii. I have to admit I thought long and hard about it because the money was so good, but in the end, I turned down the offer because I loved the autonomy and future growth potential of my job at Kuhio Mall.

With my decline of the firm's offer, Jack immediately started to cool his romancing and we both moved on to new people and adventures in a couple of months. Looking back, I have to wonder, was I an "acquisition" for the firm that was not completed?

Jack and I stayed friends, and in May, 1983, I received a telephone call from him.

"Hello Sunshine."

"Hello Handsome. What's new with Hawaii's version of Tony Manero in *Saturday Night Fever?*"

"Very Funny, Travolta would be so lucky to have my looks and dance steps."

"You graduates of the University of Spoiled Children all know the answers," I laughed.

"You know it, Baby!"

After some other pleasantries and gossip about other club members, he got serious and said,

"I told Mr. R. about your restaurant space at the Mall and he's interested in it for his newest venture. He wants to see it on Wednesday at 4 p.m. sharp. Can you accommodate him, please?"

"Absolutely."

Ronald Rewald was born September 24, 1942, making him forty-one years old at the time I met him. He appeared small in stature, about five feet eight inches tall, a little overweight and not very athletic looking. This image could have been just my perception because he was always surrounded by extremely tall, thick, black-suited Hawaiian and Samoan bodyguards. Sometimes there were four, sometimes six of them, depending on the function. He had very blue eyes and dirty red-blonde hair, which he wore longer over his ears, as was the style in the 1980's for a businessman in Honolulu. He was always impeccably dressed, wearing nothing but handmade Italian suits and English shoes.

He arrived at Kuhio Mall precisely at four o'clock in one of two, black, shiny, late-model stretch Cadillac limousines. Two guards were in the car with him, and four in the other with Jack. Mr. Rewald quickly walked through the shopping center and when we looked into the 6,000 square-foot second floor space fronting Kuhio Avenue, said to Jack,

"Yes, this will work for our first Safe House. Get the paperwork completed, Jack." He looked at me, said "Thank you," and was gone. His site visit lasted no more then fifteen minutes.

"Safe House?" I inquired, as I looked at Jack.

In true secret espionage operation, a safe house is said to be a building for hiding, or carrying out underground activities for covert agents. The original Safe House Restaurant opened for business in Milwaukee, Wisconsin, in 1966, and is still in operation. The one-of-a-kind eatery has been an icon of the city since the day it started.

The Milwaukee restaurant is a fun concept of what a real safe house must be like for spies. You need a password to get into the eatery and its concept is James Bond and CIA spy-themed. In the restaurant, there are many doors which go nowhere, and spy décor everywhere. Your wait staff are "covert agents" and they serve spy drinks like martinis that are "shaken, not stirred." The restaurant has been featured in movies like *Major League*, and numerous articles in magazines like *Time* and *People*. Even Rachel Ray did a spot in her television series on the Travel Channel, *$40 a Day*. She commented on the show, "You would have to be a CIA agent to figure this place out in one trip."

Within a week of my meeting Mr. Rewald, I received a letter of interest and a $1,000 check as a deposit for the first right of refusal on the space. Jack said they were in the process of getting a franchise agreement with the Safe House owners, and it looked like this location would be the first of several throughout Hawaii, Japan, and Australia. As soon as the agreement was signed, he would be coming to me for a lease contract.

I was excited, but when I showed Andre the letter and check; he was not.

"I have been invited to the Polo Club this Sunday. My wife is out of town, so let's go check everything out and you can introduce me to him."

"Oh Andre, it's my day off. I don't want to have to dress up and put make-up on." I lamented.

"I'll pick you up at one o'clock in the Ferrari, top down."

"Your Magnum P.I. red Ferrari! You got it, Mr. T. One o'clock it is."

I didn't know Ferraris could turn corners on a dime at 70 miles per hour, but I learned that on Sunday. When we got to the polo field, Andre asked, "Well, how did you like the ride?"

"Good, but can we go back and pick up my stomach on the way home. I think I lost it back by the Schofield Barracks turn," I said as I crawled out of the car.

"You'll be fine with a little wine," he smiled, "Now let's see who's here and meet this Mr. Rewald."

The Hawaii Polo Club is said to be one of the oldest in the United States. In 1983 it listed among its honorary members Charles, the Prince of Wales, the Sultan of Brunei, the Marquees of Waterford, and the extremely wealthy and highly connected Ricky Zobel of the Philippines. When we walked in, we found that the club had been transformed from the previous burger and beer barbecue hangout, to a mini palace with expensive overhead tenting, heavy mahogany tables and chairs, Waterford crystal goblets filled with champagne and Wedgwood china displaying food of every kind. A young chef was serving hand carved sandwiches to patrons. Three stunningly beautiful young ladies were pouring Crystal and Dom Perignon champagne to anyone within reach. There was a crowd of people, all dressed in coats and ties; the women were wearing their finest jewelry for all to see.

Over the next two hours, we met and schmoozed with all the "who's who" of Honolulu, as Andre knew all of them… and he was right; after my second glass of Crystal, my stomach found its way home. Mr. Rewald was there holding court with his ever-present bodyguards always within five feet of him.

Jack was there too, and when he saw me, he gestured for me to come. When I walked over, he bent, and with a quick kiss, handed me a small box. I opened it, and inside was an embroidered Hawaii Polo Club emblem.

"It's for your jacket. Sew it on and when you come out again to watch the matches those eunuchs over there will think you're a member of the club and let you in automatically."

"Oh Jack, that's so sweet of you. I'm so glad I called to let you know we were coming down. Thank you."

"Now don't go all goofy on me," he said with a big smile.

I took him over to meet Andre, and after a few moments he took us over to Mr. Rewald and introduced Andre to him. Within a few minutes, Mr. Rewald said something about what a great location the Mall would be for his new restaurant, and with that, turned to someone else, essentially dismissing us.

As we walked back to the main table to get something to eat, Andre said to me, "That guy is a phony."

"You think so? Everyone here tells me he is the real deal," I said.

"I don't believe so. It doesn't make sense. No one knows anything about him, or where he comes from. No one knows how he got all his money. None of my contacts on the mainland, in Asia, or Europe have ever heard of him or his company. Look how he conducts himself, with all those goons around him. Even Chris Hemmeter, who is listed as one of Forbes wealthiest Americans, doesn't act like this guy. He's a fraud, so make sure you cash that check fast. I don't have a good feeling about him."

On July 29, 1983, as I was having dinner with my parents and watching the news. Barbara Tanabe of KHON-TV, who only a few days before had scooped all the other stations with a story that the Internal Revenue Service was conducting an investigation on Ron

Rewald and his firm because of false FDIC insurance claims, was now telling her viewers he had been found alone in a hotel room at the Sheraton Waikiki Hotel with cuts to his forearms and wrists. Rewald had attempted suicide.

"Holy Moly! Andre was right." I said to Mom and Dad.

Ron Rewald was taken to the hospital and six days later, while still there, his creditors and government authorities forced Bishop Baldwin into bankruptcy. On August 8, 1983 as he was being discharged from Queen's Hospital, the police arrested him on charges of theft by deception. His bail was set at $10,000,000. He faced 400 years in prison for 98 charges of deception.

I got a call from Jack on the 10th. "Hello Sunshine. Just wanted to say aloha. I am headed to Japan for awhile."

"Will you be okay?" I asked.

"Everything will be fine. Just need to lay low until all this sorts out. Will be talking to you soon. I promise."

"Aloha Jack. I'll miss your smiling face," I said.

"Yours too, Sunshine." It was the last time I ever heard from him.

At Rewald's trial in 1984, the deputy city prosecutor, Peter Carlisle, who later became mayor of Honolulu, described Rewald as a "snake-oil salesman." Carlisle went on to say the real truth was the investment firm was a Ponzi scheme where Rewald used monies from new investors to pay interest to older ones, all the while drawing off dollars to pay for his extravagant way of life.

At the trial, it was shown everything about Rewald was a fraud; he had no personal money sources. His college degree from Marquette University was bogus, as he really had gone only to Milwaukee Area Technical College, a two-year vocational college. There was no franchise agreement for the Safe House Restaurant, although he had gone there to lunch many times when he lived in Milwaukee. He did try out for both the Cleveland Browns, where he was cut before the season started, and the Kansas City Chiefs, where he was on their practice squad for a year.

Rewald's trial started in October, 1984, and lasted for eleven weeks. He had wanted Melvin Belli as his trial lawyer, with Belli expressing an interest in defending him, but the Judge denied his request and assigned Samuel P. King, Jr., the son of the Federal Judge, and a recent law school graduate, to the case.

Rewald presented an unanticipated defense in which he claimed his business operation had been a front for the CIA, and in fact, ABC News in September, 1984, aired a two-part program supporting his statements.

During the trial, Rewald stated that he had been recruited by the agency for various operations while at college, and tried to present evidence of his CIA connections. He said the CIA told him in October, 1978, to create his company with offices throughout Asia for the purpose of providing a "cover" for covert agents in Asia. This is known in the intelligence community as "backstopping." He also went on to disclose it was never his intention to not pay his firm's investors back, but he had been waiting for reimbursements from the Agency.

The CIA denied ever knowing Rewald and filed a formal complaint with the Federal Communications Commission to seal Rewald's information. The Agency prevailed with the court and all documents and information relating to the CIA were sealed for the trial.

Rewald was convicted of mail fraud, offering securities for sale under fraudulent pretenses, transporting stolen securities in interstate commerce, failure to maintain records required by the Securities and Exchange Commission, perjury, and income tax evasion. He was sentenced to eighty years in prison and remanded to the Federal Correctional Institution on Terminal Island in California.

Sunny Wong had already pleaded guilty before Rewald's trial and was sentenced to two years in prison. When he got out, he came back to the Honolulu Club for a couple of years and continued to play racquetball with his friends. No one ever understood how he supported himself and his lifestyle.

Rewald appealed his conviction to the 9th Circuit Court of Appeals, which affirmed the District Court sentence on November 13, 1989. He then appealed to the Supreme Court of the United States in 1990, and Kenneth Starr, solicitor general at the time, who claimed that Rewald's petition to be heard by the court had not been presented in a timely manner and therefore did not merit a hearing. Rewald's petition to be heard was then refused by the court.

With all appeals exhausted, Rewald served ten years in Federal prison and was released in 1995 because, it was rumored, of a severe back injury he received from an attack in prison. His parole case file was closed in 2001. Today he lives in Los Angeles and works for a talent agency with offices in New York City, Nashville, and Beverly Hills.

You would think that was the end of the story of Ronald Rewald and Bishop Baldwin. However, in 1998, Gary Webb, a Pulitzer Prize winning investigative journalist for the San Jose Mercury News, wrote a book called "Dark Alliance" based on his 1996 "Dark Alliance" series of articles about the CIA and their links to the Contras and the crack cocaine explosion in the United States. In his book, Webb wrote how the CIA commanders were very pleased, and even gave an award to one of its agents for outstanding service in assisting with the suppression of all information about the agency in the Ron Rewald trial.

Then in 2005, Rodney Stich, a former federal investigator, wrote two books on the CIA. The first one was titled "Drugging America: A Trojan Horse," in which he wrote that Rewald and he became friends and confidants in the 1990s, and how Rewald showed him documentation of his CIA life. Stich states the CIA even had an alias for Rewald... "Winterdog." He also mentioned in this book one of the more fascinating aspects of Bishop Baldwin, which was how many of the consultants who worked for the firm were retired, high-level military people with previous connections to the agency.

The second book, entitled, "Disavow: A CIA Saga of Betrayal," Stich, along with his co-author, T. Conan Russell, wrote that Rewald, through different federal agencies, was made to be the scapegoat to conceal the true reason for the existence of Bishop Baldwin. According to the authors, the real reason for Bishop Baldwin was simple: to provide a cover for CIA operatives and agents and funnel money for the covert activities these agents were working on at the time.

Before there was Bernie Madoff, there was Ron Rewald. Was Mr. Rewald a fraud, or was he a covert spy for the CIA? Did the CIA really set up his firm? Or was it all a very large Ponzi scheme?

What we do know is that $22,000,000 from four hundred of Hawaii's trusting people was spent on a lavish lifestyle for Rewald. Some people were ruined because of him, like many with Madoff. His multi-million dollar home, as well as all his other possessions, were auctioned off to pay his investors. The house still stands, although the paddle tennis court is gone due to the widening of Kalanianaole Highway in 1990. I turned over the $1,000 deposit to the bankruptcy trustee and the space for his Safe House was leased to a nightclub in 1985.

From time to time, however, I still wonder what ever happened to Jack Madison. Why did he immediately leave for Japan when

Rewald's empire collapsed? I checked a few years ago and there was no record of a Jack Madison attending or graduating from the University of Southern California during the time he said he went there.

So who really was Jack Madison?

CHAPTER TWENTY-FOUR

My Paradise Became My Hades

Stormy seas were brewing around my ship in my fourth year at the mall, and my Paradise became my Hades.

In 1985, Hotel Corporation of the Pacific was planning on launching its new name, ASTON Hotels & Resorts, using Andre's initials of "AST," and marketing it like other international hotel players ala Hilton and Sheraton. The company was now hosting more than 500,000 guests per year with both the condominium and hotel trade, and with this branding, it could combine both operations under one common name.

With the name change and new programs underway, Andre no longer had time to personally supervise me. The mall also was now losing only about $10,000 per month and was expected to breakeven before the year was out, so it was no longer an issue for him.

Edward had taken a leave of absence because he had desperately fallen in love with a tenant of the mall and was now in the midst of a very bitter divorce from his wife of 25 years. Morris Sidebottom,* who had been a loyal staff manager to Andre, but who had never been in an operations position before, was chomping at the bit for a chance to be "a real manager" and asked for a chance to take over the mall. Andre agreed, and at first I thought he was an excellent choice.

Morris and I had been friends, learning to ski together in Tahoe, but what I failed to notice was that Morris and Doris Ghoul,* one of my staff members, were attracted to each other and had been having an affair for sometime. For him, it was love at first sight, and his 35-year marriage was over the first time Doris walked into his office. My new boss and my assistant were now a couple, and decisions were being made concerning me during pillow talk conversations between them.

I assumed I had undying loyalty from my team, and particularly Doris. I met her when she was a twenty-year-old student at the University of Hawaii, working part time at a company I dealt with occasionally. We continued to be good friends for many years and I thought of her as my little sister. She was smart and clever, and as soon as I had the opportunity, I hired her to work with me. I made sure she attended classes to improve her real estate knowledge, and I got her licensed because I looked at her as someone I could trust as I climbed up the corporate ladder. I was very generous and continually rewarded her, along with others on my team, with bonuses, gifts, trips, and education as a reward for their good work. However, I soon realized when passion and obsession combine, friendship and loyalty often become victims of the fervor.

With Morris and Doris a team, it became obvious there was a zealousness to prove to everyone that they had the ability to manage operations and there would be no mercy for me. At first it started with Doris taking over management of the maintenance and security departments. Soon all correspondence went directly to her, rather than me. Finally, I was not allowed to see the financial reports or have any conversations with existing tenants. Within ninety days, my only purpose was leasing, and that slowed down as most of the mall was now occupied.

To make matters worse, Morris started to micro-manage me on every level. I was called into his office for morning and afternoon meetings to discuss my attitude and told to keep records of who I spoke to and when. I had to report to the mall precisely at 7:30 a.m. and stay until 5:30 p.m. Monday through Friday, and from 8:00 a.m. to 2:00 p.m. on Saturday, even though Doris continued to saunter in at 9:00 a.m. everyday.

Finally, on a Saturday five days before Christmas, Morris came into my office and sat down across from me. I knew I was in trouble the moment he grinned at me. He was smiling with those long yellow teeth and squirrelly eyes I had grown to hate.

"I have decided to fire you, but I just haven't decided when." He said, smirking as he looked at me.

I had saved up some money and was in escrow on my first home after renting for eight years. I had already moved in with an early occupancy agreement as all contingencies had been removed and I was closing on it two days after the New Year. He knew this and seemed to know what I was thinking.

"I hope you will at least let me live through the holidays." I said, almost in a whisper.

"Well, we'll have to see how I feel and how you perform for me,"

He actually giggled as he said this, knowing his power over me was now complete.

He kept me on through the holiday season, I don't know why, but I think he was probably too busy with parties and romancing Doris. In early January we met and I told him he had won and I was done, but needed a severance package and time to look for another job. I was surprised how generous he was, maybe it was because of Andre, or maybe there was a fear of a wrongful termination lawsuit. I left in February without fanfare or acknowledgement from anyone on my former team, as most of them were terrified of losing their jobs. Loyalty was essential and absolute for Morris and Doris.

When I went back to the mall three weeks later to pick up some mail, I no longer had parking privileges and was followed around the shopping center by the new maintenance manager. He was on his walkie-talkie, constantly reporting on my every move and conversations to the management office upstairs.

As I drove out of the parking lot, I noticed all the vines on the main building's walls that I had planted to give the shopping center the impression of being part of International Marketplace had been removed. My time in power was over, and my period of influence completed at Kuhio Mall. I was now a nobody, starting all over again.

CHAPTER TWENTY-FIVE

The Legacies Of Dad And Mom

I love cigars. Not the small ones like panatelas, but the big double coronas, just like the Cuban women in the Anthony Bourdain episode of *No Reservations* on the Travel Channel. I smoke about three to four a week in the mornings or evenings when I walk my dog. The aroma and taste touch my very soul and when I smoke, I always think about my Dad and Mom.

My Dad taught me to really enjoy big, fine cigars. My Mom made sure I smoked like a lady, and didn't spit in public. Some of the fondest memories of my parents are when I was just beginning my real estate career. The three of us would often sit around the dining table after dinner, smoking, drinking a few, and discussing current events in the real estate business here and abroad.

My Dad, Thomas Athanasios Sofos, was born in a small village outside of Corinth, Greece. After his father died of pneumonia, his young, widowed mother needed a new life and came to America via Ellis Island with her two year old son.

My Mom, Catherine Bassilika, was born in St. Louis, Missouri, but was raised in Athens, Greece, from the time she was five. English was the second language for both of my parents. Together they were strongly of "the old country" in their disciplines, but very much of the new world in their desires for the best life possible for themselves and their family.

Dad had won an appointment to the United States Naval Academy, Class of 1944. As a Naval aviator during World War II, he was seriously wounded in the Pacific, retired as a Lieutenant at the age of twenty-five, and decided to remain in Honolulu. He was a man who loved the sea and the romance of island life with beach barbecues, girls in swimsuits, and Hawaii's national libation, *Okolehao*.

Mom came back to America after the Nazis invaded Greece, and did not see her mother again for twenty-three years. On her own from the age of sixteen, with the help of a guardian and the Greek Church in St. Louis, she went to school, became an accountant, and in 1943 landed a job as an auditor for the Pearl Harbor Naval Exchange. At the age of twenty-one she came to Honolulu on an LST transport, and the morning she arrived, was on the deck drinking coffee. As the sun rose, exposing the Waianae Mountains, she told herself she knew she had found her new home, as the mountains and coastline reminded her so much of Greece.

On February 6, 1946, she met my Dad at a cocktail party. Someone asked my Dad if he wanted to meet a Greek girl, and by saying he did, I'm sure he didn't imagine, in his wildest dreams, that three weeks later he would be saying, "I do."

As he walked up to her, she was playing Beethoven's *Fur Elise* on the host's baby grand piano. She was wearing a tight fitting, sky-blue, silk dress to match her eyes…nylons, four-inch black stilettos, and red lipstick to go with her recent manicure. She was twenty-three years old, with Rita Hayworth red, shoulder-length hair, and a figure to beat the best of them.

He said something glib in Greek to her, and she most certainly was not impressed. This instantly intrigued him because everyone, particularly the ladies, were so charmed by the young, perfectly groomed, polished, and very handsome cigar-smoking, twenty-five year old Annapolis graduate.

That night they talked, danced, kissed, and argued, and then walked away; but three days later he was at her doorstep with roses in his hand. On February 14th at the Willows Restaurant in Moilili, he proposed and she said, "Yes." They would have been married on the 26th but Mom couldn't get off work, so on March 1st they became husband and wife by way of Joseph Bright, a Mormon Bishop, who was the grandfather of the iconic Hawaiian musician and singer, Teresa Bright, and spent their honeymoon at the Laie Hotel. They married in the Orthodox Church eight months later in Maryland.

On their twenty-fifth wedding anniversary in 1971, Mom wrote in her diary, "Within three days of seeing each other we knew we were to marry. I can't help but think our marriage was arranged in heaven." They were together for over fifty-two years before his death in 1998.

The first years of their marriage were difficult because, in those days, finding work was hard for G.I.s coming back into the main stream of America. Dad couldn't find work as an electrical engineer, the field he had earned a degree in at the Academy. He became a liquor salesman, then a car salesman. Mom and he even went back to his mother's home in Annapolis, Maryland, to see if he could get a job through the family, but there was no work there either. They moved to San Francisco, and for a year operated a restaurant on Geary Street, near Union Square. They gave up the business when thugs, looking for protection money, threatened to beat them and destroy the restaurant.

Finally, at Mom's insistence, they moved back to Hawaii. Mom knew Dad had a lot of insight and convinced him that they should start their own business. During the war, Dad had acquired a small parcel of Waikiki land for $5,000 with a down payment of $2,500 from a nest egg he had won during a night of poker-playing on his ship. He arranged for the balance to be paid out of his monthly salary and retirement pay over the next five years.

After working long and hard with lenders, and collateralizing his Navy pension, State Savings, a small, local savings and loan, gave them the financing they needed to start their company, TASCO Realty and Contractors, Inc., (Thomas A. Sofos and Company, Realty and Contractors, Inc.) They then proceeded to build their first project on the small lot. The "Sofos Building" was built in 1948, and remains standing today. Downstairs was a retail store fronting Kalakaua Avenue; their offices were located upstairs along with six apartments.

For the next seventeen years, they expanded their business and family. My Dad was a true visionary, and together they built houses and apartments in Waialae-Kahala, Waikiki, Kaneohe, and Kalihi. During this time, they also produced four children, my three older brothers and me. As the baby of the family, I went everywhere with my parents…collecting rents with Dad, and walking on job sites with my Barbie in one hand and my Mom's hand in the other, holding me steady so I wouldn't fall down on the rocks.

Life was good, but hard for them; the contracting/development business has a lot of ups and downs, feasts or famines, and is highly stressful with constant worries about financing and sales. Dad had his first heart attack at the age of thirty-five, and Mom had kidney stones removed on three separate occasions before she was forty.

In 1958, Dad and Mom were awarded the development rights of Waialae Nui Ridge by Bishop Estate. It was to be the first ridge project of Honolulu, with breathtaking views of the Pacific Ocean that only hikers had previously been able to enjoy. The houses were designed by the internationally famous architect, Vladimir Ossipoff, and included three and four bedrooms with prices starting at $28,000. It was their biggest undertaking and they were thrilled.

However, the blue rock, which permeated the mountain, proved to be their nemesis. With costs soaring for the climb up the ridge, dynamite, which was legal to use in those days, was the only solution to excavate the hill in order to make level areas for building homes. The explosions were constant daily occurrences, and people began to take them as commonplace. Mom and I often walked the most recent exploded areas with hard hats as she surveyed the day's progress.

On August 17, 1962 at 1:30 p.m., like a Greek tragedy Homer might have written, disaster struck. My parents' sub-contractors had been dynamiting the construction area that morning to install sewer lines for the new subdivision. In the early afternoon, a little eight-year old girl climbed into a drainage canal some three hundred feet away and one hundred fifty feet below the building site.

She had never visited the spot before, but went there to collect *halekoa* seeds to make bracelets with her cousin and a friend. Somehow, at that very moment, a large boulder, estimated to weigh over five hundred pounds, was dislodged, sped down the hill, bounced up and over the concrete rail used for the ditch, and landed directly on the little girl. She was instantly crushed to death.

Her father stated in an interview with the *Honolulu Star Bulletin* two days later that he did not blame anyone for the freak accident. He said of her death, "It was a million-to-one chance."

When Dad and Mom heard about the accident, they were devastated; it was like their very souls had been destroyed with the little girl's death. Both of them went into a depression that everyone who knew them had never seen before. The happy-go-lucky, always-optimistic personalities they were noted for were silenced. Within three years of the little girl's death, they transferred their development rights for the ridge to another builder, sold our house in Kahala, and moved to our country house on Kaneohe Bay.

For the next three years, they did almost no business. During this time, with my brothers in boarding school on the Big Island of Hawaii, and Dad not working, he and I spent a lot of time in the ocean, fishing and boating on the windward side. This was when I developed my great love for the sea, much like my father's passion.

It was also in these years that Mom and Dad became heavily involved in establishing a Greek Orthodox Church here in Hawaii. Looking back now, I believe the church became their corporal atonement for the tragic death of the little girl. Slowly, they both started to emerge from the abyss of their sadness, and with three other families, they became the founding godparents of the church.

A permanent home for the church was established in 1968 in an old house located on Old Pali Place in Nuuanu, and was named in part for Dad's mother, Helen. In 1988, the Church moved to its present home at 930 Lunalilo Street in Makiki, and is now called the Saints Constantine and Helen Greek Orthodox Cathedral of the Pacific.

With the church founded, their energy and spirits were uplifted and rejuvenated. They sold our house in Kaneohe and we moved back to Honolulu. Dad started up a real estate brokerage business and began buying and selling properties for individuals and himself. Being the quintessential salesman, life for us was good once more, and traveling the world became one of their special joys.

By the time I was at Kuhio Mall, Dad and Mom were semi-retired, with Dad completing one or two sales transactions per year, and Mom working at H & R Block during tax preparation season to get out of the house. I kept them involved in my life at the Mall and they came to all our Christmas parties and picnics.

They both knew my staff and often walked the property with me. They also knew about Morris and Doris.

The day Morris told me he was going to fire me, but just didn't know when, I went over to have dinner with my parents. We sat at the dining table as always, and I poured out my heart. What do I do now? Where do I go from here? Christmas was five days away.

Dad's first reaction was, "He's a prick and needs a good punch in the mouth and a swift kick in the balls." Then, after a long moment, he said, "Why don't you work for yourself for awhile. You've said you want to be free and independent since your KACOR days."

Then Mom broke in: "Look, Dad and I talked about this, I can do your books and set up your accounting. You can work out of your apartment."

"Where am I going to get clients? Who's going to work with me?" I quietly asked.

"Sister," which was his pet name for me and how he always addressed me when he wanted my attention, "you're smarter than almost all of the cadets together currently at Army." He hated West Point with a vengeance. "Now figure it out! You can always get a job, but a job is all you will get. And who knows if your next boss will be an even bigger asshole than this one. This may be your time. Work with your mother and do it."

"If you fail, you fail, but if you don't try, you will never know," was my mother's comment.

"At this point, you have nothing to lose," was Dad's last remark before going off to bed.

Mom and I sat there drinking coffee. With my head hanging so low it was almost touching the table, she said,

"Stephany, sit up. You're defeated before you've even started. You can do this or you can fail, it's up to you. Your Dad has a good reputation in town. His word and his handshake are his contracts. You have a good family name and it will help carry you through this time."

Over the next few weeks, with the end coming to my days at Kuhio Mall, Dad, Mom, and I had more cigars and dinners together, and each time we talked, they told me stories of their days in business and what to do and what not to do. Who to know and who to avoid. Their support was unwavering and their histories of tragedies and triumphs were eye-opening. Those evening dinner conversations were the greatest business lessons of my life, and with their encouragement and good names, I stepped into the world of self-employment and have never looked back.

One recent evening, my neighbor, a professional writer, saw me walking with a cocktail in one hand, Nalu's leash in the other, puffing on a stogie. He looked at me and said,

"Stephany, you would make a great character in a book, but I don't think anyone would really believe it."

I smiled and said to him, "If you think I'm a personality, you should have met my parents."

CHAPTER TWENTY-SIX

On My Own And Terrified

With my severance pay I did absolutely nothing for the first couple of months but read books on the beach, surf, play tennis and racquetball. I had no idea what I would do with myself, or if I should listen to Mom and Dad.

After a while, I began to make job inquiries around town, but some people wouldn't take my telephone calls, and others would see me on the street, or at the Honolulu Club, and literally turn their backs to me as I approached them. After another four weeks of job-hunting, and finding nothing that would pay me what I wanted, I made the decision to go solo.

I was now on my own and terrified, but there was always my parents' constant encouragement, my brother Steven's counseling, and a few friends in Waikiki who were willing to give me a chance to show my abilities. As Alexander Haig once said, "If you have a firm set of ideas, if you want to make a difference, sometimes you've got to be controversial," and being self-employed, I knew I needed something that would separate me from the pack. I set four goals for myself.

The first was: since I hated dressing up because of the constant heat in Honolulu, and with flat feet, which made it painful for me to wear high heels, I would have to find a "look" that was clean, but casual. I settled on brightly colored short or long sleeve Ralph Lauren shirts, starched and ironed blue jeans or tailored walking shorts, and sneakers to match the color of my shirts. I had quite the ensemble; teal shirt, teal shoes, red shirt, red shoes, pink shirt, pink shoes, and so on. I decorated myself with standard real estate agents' accessories: Rolex steel and gold watch, gold bracelets, large hoop earrings, and a gold chain necklace or string of pearls.

My second goal was to sell my research on Waikiki properties, something no one had done before. I had been collecting all the leasing and sales information for every Waikiki transaction since 1982, and I would make my data available for a fee. Retailers and landlords alike always want to know what the competition is doing, and I was able to tell them for a good amount of money.

The third goal was to market myself as the most knowledgeable Waikiki real estate broker in the islands. I decided to get a small office in the area and make my presence known.

I started off slowly, talking to all the Waikiki landlords, then the tenants, showing everyone I was willing to work on their deal no matter how small. The vendors and tenants started to recognize me as I walked around in my brightly colored shirts and sneakers, and introduced me to other retailers and friends. "Hi Polo Lady, Miss Stephany!" I often heard as I walked through the different centers. Within six weeks, I had completed a couple of leasing transactions in

Waikiki. One was for a Subway franchise, the other for an office at the Waikiki Trade Center.

My fourth goal was to find a mentor. My brother, Steven, had found Harry Weinberg, the real estate billionaire tycoon, to be his teacher. Harry was instrumental in schooling Steven in what to look for in undervalued assets and master ground leasing. Steven often brought me along on visits with Harry at his penthouse apartment on Ohua Avenue in Waikiki. For a man who had emigrated from Europe as a child, quit school at the age of twelve to help support his family, and then, through hard work and smarts, acquired immense wealth, Henry Weinberg was actually a simple and modest person. He had been a ferocious negotiator and businessman when he was younger, but by the time I knew him he lived a Spartan existence, mainly focusing on building the Harry and Jeanette Weinberg Foundation that would one day give his money to the poor after he and his wife died. He was a taskmaster with Steven at times, but with me, he was one of the most gracious gentlemen I ever met.

My mentor was Donald H. Graham, Jr., the father of Ala Moana Shopping Center, which was built in 1959 and remains today the largest outdoor shopping center in America. I got to know Don when I was at Discovery Bay Shopping Center, and through the many functions of the International Council of Shopping Centers. He was smart and creative, and always had a positive word for me.

Sometimes being a mentor is just about listening to your student's problems and offering words of encouragement. That is what Don did for me. We would lunch at the Tahitian Lanai once or twice a month, which coincidently, was where Harry Weinberg often dined. He would tell me his ideas for retail and development. He once told me the genius of Ala Moana Shopping Center had not been the design, but the fact that they were able to concurrently build all four components of development to feed off each other at the same time. "Retail" was the shopping center, "Residential" was the 1350 Ala Moana condominium across Piikoi Street, "Office" was the Ala Moana office building with the rotating La Ronde restaurant on the top, and "Recreational" was Ala Moana Beach Park across Ala Moana Boulevard. All of this was completed in 1959, and changed the face of Honolulu forever: I thought the concept was absolutely brilliant.

Often I lamented to Don about being a "Career Gal," and how life was hard with money coming is ebbs and flows. But he always told me the same thing: be respectful of others, speak the truth, be mindful of doing a good job, and with these concepts always in mind, I would be okay no matter what life chose to deal me.

For the first five years of self-employment, all my work centered on leasing and data research in Waikiki, and the retail market in general. But with competition growing, I needed to expand into other areas. Over the next several years, I expanded my business while maintaining my Waikiki presence. I sold a couple of small commercial condominiums, one of which was a gun shop and the other a sex shop. I started doing office leases in the downtown financial district, leased a few warehouses in Kaneohe and Kakaako, went back into the residential market and sold a few single-family homes and condominiums and sold raw land to a national fast food franchise. I assisted in leasing a new location in Waikiki to one of the largest international retailers in the world, even became a day manager for a residential apartment complex.

If someone was willing to work with me, I would do the labor to keep the cash flowing, and to keep me from looking for a job again. I called myself a "Jackie of all trades and a mistress of none," to paraphrase the old saying, and my friends dubbed me, "Consultant

Woman." I became quite adept at moving from one aspect of the business to the other, and back again, which is what I still do today.

This moving from phase to phase of the business gave me insight into the different facets of real estate, honed my skills, and taught me lessons I needed to be a good consultant. This has been fundamental to how I work in the business.

First, I learned that residential real estate is all about emotions. How does the home make your client feel? Happy, secure, worried, etc? Some deals have been made or broken by whether the property has electric or gas appliances, or glass doors or plastic shower curtains. And sometimes you cannot reason with your buyer or seller because he or she, for whatever rationale, has become so involved with the property that they become obsessed with it.

Second, in retail real estate, retail is also about emotions, particularly if the merchant is local. Logistics and location are the most important for them because usually the family is involved with the decision-making and plan to work in the business, be it store or restaurant.

Third, in warehousing and office space, while location is important, the main focus is about the numbers, and can they truly afford the space.

Fourth, in consulting, you must always protect your intellectual property from being stolen by others in the business. When I learned, after an arbitration, that an appraiser, under his name, had published in the *Honolulu Advertiser* a marketing study I had written, I was furious. He had not even taken the time to change the format I had used for my exhibits. I called the attorney involved in the hearing and he said I should take it as a compliment that my work was good enough to be "lifted" and know that I had now arrived. I decided then and there that all reports were mine and after I received the payment for my work, I would publish the non-confidential information from my studies on my own so no one could jump on my work and claim it for their purposes.

Fifth, what I learned concerned the media; Malia Mattoch, then a reporter and weekend anchor for KHON TV2, read a story about me in *Pacific Business News* and called me for my very first television interview. She cautioned me to be truthful and told me, if I did not know something, to say I did not know, but not to make things up to look good. Our meeting led to other journalists working with me and seeking my opinion as a real estate expert.

What I have observed from working with reporters over the years is that the fundamental issue for them is that they demand honesty and can smell a liar a mile away. They despise fibbers because if a reporter uses false information, this can kill their own credibility and can even get them fired. I tell people when talking to the media, never, ever lie…as Malia said to me, either you know, or don't know.

If you can't give them the information they want, just say so; don't fabricate answers. They respect that, and if they catch someone lying to them, God have mercy on that person's soul because the news people will not.

CHAPTER TWENTY-SEVEN

The Greatest Job In The World

By 1994 I had been on my own as a real estate broker and consultant for over eight years when I received a telephone call from Ann Bouslog. Ann and I had met years before, during a summer college break, when she worked for a group of architects who leased office space at the Merchandise Mart. Ann graduated from Cornell with a Ph.D. in Sociology and went on to become one of Hawaii's directors for the real estate division of KPMG, an international consulting company. She had hired me from time to time over the years as a sub-consultant when her group needed specific expertise in the retail market. Over the years, we became friends and she was someone I admired. She was always calm, regardless of the deadlines she had to meet. She could move mountains with her quiet charm and brilliance.

"Stephany, I am going to take night classes at the University of Hawaii to become an appraiser and I think you should join me," the now- pregnant Ann suggested.

"Why? I have enough initials after my name already," I replied.

"Well, after the savings and loan mess of the last few years the federal government is requiring all real estate appraisers to be licensed and I believe this will give both of us an edge in our consultancies."

"Annie, do you know the difference between an appraiser and an accountant?" I queried.

"No, what?"

"An appraiser is someone who desperately wanted to be an accountant, but unfortunately did not have enough personality to do so. And you know accountants are the most boring, least humorous people in the world. We will be drowsing and snoring after the first hour of class," I said.

"Come on, it'll be fun. We can pick out names for the baby. We can eat chocolate candy bars and drink coffee from the vending machines, and we may even learn something useful," she gently, but firmly said.

"I don't know. I'm doing okay, but I still need to watch my dimes and it's expensive." I retorted.

"We can work that out, we have some work coming up for you and those fees should cover all your costs."

"And," she went on, "at six months pregnant, I want someone I know there with me at night. I don't want to be in class alone for the next three months and worry that if the baby decides to come early I'll be without someone I know to help me." These were the days before cellular telephones were commonplace.

"Geez, you'll make me feel guilty if I say no." I retorted.

"Good, then no is not an option. Classes start April 20th and go through July. I'll fax you an application." And with that, she hung up.

"What? Wait? Now what did I just agree to and how am I going to pay for this?"

I was unenthusiastic, but in the end, I went with her for two reasons: one was that I agreed an appraisal license would look good on my resume. The second was, I really did have these thoughts she would "pop" in class and I would feel terrible that I hadn't been there for her. Again, that Catholic guilt was rearing its head.

The classes were actually quite interesting. We passed the courses, the four-hour computer examination, and the peer review committee, who reviewed our previous reports. Ann and I became the only two people in the entire state to ever become certified general appraisers through the consultancy side of it. Almost all appraisers usually complete an apprenticeship to learn the business for a minimum of three years. Our licenses gave us the right to appraise all types of commercial, business, and residential real estate. Today, you also need a bachelor's degree from an accredited college to even sit for the test.

The late Ray Lesher, our instructor, along with Bob Vernon, were two of the most respected appraisers ever to work in Hawaii, and Ray told us, the day we received our licenses, to go to Brooks Brothers and open an account, as we were now "People of Independent Opinion." We were to be conservative on every level and carefully choose our words when speaking to people, because once you gave an opinion on something, it was an appraisal, and you had better be able to back up your viewpoint.

Ann was right, and as soon as I received my license I was immediately treated differently by people in and out of the real estate business, and a whole new world opened up for me in both the commercial and residential arenas.

I started working with attorneys and consulting firms and continued to expand my business. However, no matter how hard you try, commercial and business valuation, while it pays well, is not the most exciting work in the world. Commercial appraisals consist of numbers, formulas, cost breakdowns, market analyses, discounted cash flows, and detailed descriptions of the properties. All appraisers are under strict federal guidelines as to how reports are presented, and if you have seen one warehouse, walkup apartment building, or small office building, you have seen them all. Retail and shopping center work is more interesting because of the stores, especially when you get to spend all day watching people to see what they buy.

On the other hand, residential appraisal is truly fascinating because you see how people live everyday. In Hawaii, with our multi-ethnic cultures, after a time you get to know the particular idiosyncrasies of certain ethnic groups, and who lives in which house, just by driving down a street. It can definitely be said that not everyone is the same, but more often then not, there are certain similarities.

When inspecting properties, one can readily see these tendencies up close, and it's fun for me to see if my observations are correct.

Here are some of the interesting commonalities I have found over the years. Many local Japanese families have chain link fences and concrete everywhere, with the exception of a small area so their Chihuahuas, Papillions, Pomeranians, or Bichon Frises can poop. They have stacks of old newspapers, cans, and plastic bottles in neat piles in the carport to take to the recycler. They spend the money from recycling on a vacation trip to Las Vegas.

They almost all drive a Toyota Camry, Lexus, or some form of Honda. Most of them are concerned about me getting enough to drink because of our hot weather, and always offer me bottled water whenever I come to inspect their homes.

Native Hawaiian families tend to always have one or two pit bulls wandering around the yard, or tied right in front of the entrance to the house. There is usually a mango tree on the property, and an old car in the front that every neighbor kid has worked on, or is presently working on. The cars are often vintage, from the 1930s to the 1980s. The carport or garage is the recreation room for the family and most of the neighborhood, and many in the immediate area are more than likely related. The garage is stocked with a refrigerator and television, there's a barbecue by the side yard, and a big table with chairs in the center for the weekend *pau hana* (after work) parties. There are usually children of all ages running around, especially if I'm measuring the property. Hawaiians gravitate to big cars and trucks like Lincoln Navigators, Dodge Rams, Chevy Suburbans, or Toyota Titans, and are always generous with their food.

The Chinese have the most expensive houses when first purchased. Detail is often exquisite, with intricate woodcarvings with inlaid dragons and lions. However, once purchased, this is frequently the last time any money is put into the house. Chinese like to have their money working for them, and using dollars for maintaining a house they live in does not create the velocity and volume of income they want.

Many times I have inspected these homes, which are now twenty-five to forty years older, and have remained in a time warp from a past era. The properties are often in great need of repair and modernization. The owners almost always ask me how much I am charging for my report, to reconfirm the bank is not overcharging them. The younger men drive Porsches, AMG Mercedes, or BMW M5s. Their wives drive Mercedes or Lexus. They rarely have pets and almost never offer me anything to eat or drink.

Filipinos never live alone and almost always have three or four generations living under one roof. As they become wealthier, they go vertical and build second stories, with what I call "Imelda Marcos balconies" which are arched, with rounded railings so they can wave from up above to the neighbors below, as affluent Filipinos do in their home country. They are constantly cooking, maybe because so many people are living there and everyone is on a different work schedule.

When I tell them my name, they almost always ask me, "Sofos, you Samoan?" When I tell them I'm Greek, most don't know what this ethnicity is because the majority are born in the Philippines and not familiar with European countries, and they say to me, "Is that like Portugee?" Portuguese, as most people know, are from the Iberian peninsula and are of European ethnicity. Hawaii's first Portuguese immigrants came from Madeira and the Azores in the nineteenth century to work on the sugar and pineapple plantations. They brought with them the ukulele, the stringed instrument that became the symbol for Hawaiian music. Arthur Godfrey, in the 1950s, and Israel Kamakawiwo'ole in the 1980s and 1990s popularized it throughout the world. However, because they were plantation workers, and not of American or British lineage, they were not considered truly *haole* (Caucasian) by the local population. Portuguese are still mostly regarded as a separate racial group. So when I tell them Portuguese and Greeks are *haoles*, I always get the same comment, "Sistah, I don't know about Greeks, but Portugee is Portugee and they are not *haole*!

If Filipinos own animals, they are usually chickens for the eggs and fresh meat. The wealthy, established ones usually drive BMWs and Mercedes. If they are recent transplants, the wives ride in older Mercedes, and the husbands, Mini-Vans or smaller trucks. They usually offer me fresh fruit, *leche flan*, or fried *lumpia* when I go to their homes to inspect, and always caution me not eat too much because of the high calories and to protect my health.

Portuguese are by far the cleanest people on the earth, and you can literally eat off their floors. The Catholic guilt is strong and everything, including their closets, dogs, cats, and grandchildren, are organized, scrubbed, and washed. Their lawns are meticulous and they always have very fat and happy *poi* (mixed-breed) dogs. Most drive mini-vans or Toyota Camrys. They often ask me to sit down while they make coffee or tea and offer an assortment of homemade cookies and cakes that are waiting on the dining table.

Mainland *haoles* who have recently located to Hawaii usually have huge, oversized furniture and high, lava rock walls. They are all big on privacy and security. Most are accustomed to large houses with expansive lawns, and have a difficult time dealing with our small lots and postage size dwellings. Often they will have a king-size bed in a room only big enough for a queen, which makes it difficult to move around.

They always insist on walking me through the house, making sure I notice every renovation that was ever made, because I believe they do not think an appraiser has the ability to see the true value of their home improvements. Mainlanders usually have happy golden or Labrador retrievers and a couple of cats for pets. They drive mini-vans, Ford Explorers, or Chevy Suburbans. They often offer me bottled water.

Local Haoles almost all live either in east Oahu or Kailua, where President Obama, or, as his Punahou schoolmates like to call him, "Our Barry," spends his Christmas holidays. They like to speak pidgin to me, so I know they are "*keiki o ka aina*" which means literally, a child of the land, or someone born in Hawaii.

Many are into water sports and look it, with their weathered and leathery, lean, fit faces and bodies. Their large collections of one-man canoes, stand up boards, and surfboards are housed in every nook and cranny. Their kitchens have the mandatory built-in wine coolers next to the refrigerators for their eclectic collection of red wine. "Red wine is so good for overall health," they always remind me.

When we first meet, they ask me the same question, which is, "Where did you go to high school?" When I tell them St. Andrew's Priory, they are truly surprised and say, "What, I thought you go Punahou?" Then they launch into their glory days of high school football or homecoming stories of the burning of the "P."

Most own Portuguese waterdogs or Labrador retrievers, and all the men drive Toyota Tacomas, Toyota Titans, or Ford 150 trucks, while their wives drive high-end SUVs, Range Rovers, Land Rovers, BMWs, or Mercedes. They usually do not offer me anything to drink or eat, which could be since they are so into their fitness regimes there is no food around the house, or maybe it's because I am just not into high school reminiscing.

CHAPTER TWENTY-EIGHT

Beware Of The Weirdos!

The residential appraisal world has been a pleasant experience for me, for the most part, and I've met many wonderful people and been in some very lovely homes. I have gone to places far and wide that I would never have imagined, if not for someone calling for my expertise.

However, there have been six particular encounters that continue to haunt me even after decades in the business. The people and circumstances involved have irrevocably forever changed me as a person.

THE MORTGAGE BROKER-HINDU-HAOLES
OF ORCHIDLAND

During the height of the sub-prime mortgage market in the mid 2000s, when almost anyone could get a loan, mortgage brokers often sent appraisers to some very odd properties. When I had to go some place I was unfamiliar with, or when I was alone on a strange property, I usually felt uncomfortable.

One of these incidents occurred when a hippie girl and her husband, who had tattoos all over his face, picked me up at the Hilo Airport. They were the mortgage solicitors for a Honolulu mortgage broker based in Keaau, a town ten miles south of Hilo. I had never met them before and when I got into their dirty, heavily dented, broken-down, ancient van with baby stuff everywhere to keep their four children occupied, I started to get a bit concerned. They were dressed all in black, in full Indian saris and turbans. They were followers of the Hindu faith, even through they both were blue-eyed, blond Caucasians, born and raised in Southern California. As we drove, I noticed she too was tattooed on much of her face and arms and they both had more than one piecing on their bodies. When I asked them why they had tattoos on their faces, they looked at each other, and then the husband said,

"So we never have to work for 'The Man'. The tattoos make sure we are forced to work for ourselves."

We drove in silence for the next thirty minutes and I thought, well it's a look, but couldn't a big note on the refrigerator door work just the same, without the pain?

"Okay, just where are we going?" I said finally.

They both looked at each other, then she turned, and ever so sweetly smiled said, "Orchidland."

Orchidland is in the deepest part of the Puna rainforest on the southeast side of the Big Island of Hawaii, and the best way to describe it is to say it's the Wild West, Hawaiian style. It has the highest rate of ex-convicts living in any particular geographic location in the state, and residents live off the land, often growing exotic plants, fruits, and *"pakalolo"* (marijuana) for their livelihood.

Many of the people living in or around the area carry big knives, guns, and have large bully dogs guarding their property. They don't like strangers and become extremely unhappy if one drives onto their land, regardless of whether or not they are lost. I've been told it could be extremely dangerous to run out of gas in the neighborhood, particularly at night. There are many squatters living in ramshackle huts and tents and a lot of burnt-out cars on the sides of the roads. Wild dogs, horses, and cats, all of which have been dumped in the forest by their former owners, and feral pigs, freely roam the area. The county roads are often full of huge potholes, with no lights or signs. Police, fire, and rescue services are almost nonexistent, and when you move there you must be self sustaining or you won't be able to survive.

When we finally arrived at the house and its three acres bordering on the Puna Forest Reserve, the owners came out to greet us with their children. They were extremely polite, and very gracious.

They were transplanted mainland *haoles* who had come to Orchidland looking for freedom from traditional American society. In their mid-thirties, they had five children, and another one on the way. All the little ones had been born on the property with the help of a midwife. Everyone was tall, but very thin, with a hungry look in his or her eyes. They were refinancing their property because there was very little money to go around, and as a carpenter, the husband found only so much work available. The wife was not bringing in any income, but was home-schooling the children and taking care of their "garden," which was finally about to be harvested after two long years. They were hoping to sell some of the yield for food and living expenses.

The garden, which measured about a half acre, was full of three-foot tall *pakalolo* plants. It was not on their land, they were quick to point out, but in the Reserve. However, the only way to get to the plants was through their property, because of a stream and densely thick forest in back of the patch. They were planning on cutting the plants in the next week because strangers were coming around and they had chased several off their property in the past few months.

With all this information, I thought they were peculiar to say the least, but when I walked through their home, I noticed there was only one bed in the entire house. When I asked about the lack of beds, I was told that, because of their religion, everyone from their teenagers to the baby, all slept in the same bed. I now knew I was totally out of my comfort zone.

As I walked near the large marijuana plants and processed all the conversations in my head, everyone could see I was getting a bit jumpy and tried to put me at ease. However, it was getting dark and I was miles from civilization. I ignored everybody and worked quickly because I don't know if it was a hallucination, but I swear I kept hearing a banjo and guitar dueling in the distance, and I wanted to get back on the plane as quickly as possible before someone could say to me, like in the movie, *Deliverance,* "squeal like a pig."

Not long after my visit, I heard the federal government moved in and destroyed all remnants of the garden.

THE SEAMSTRESS AND HER SON

I never actually met the seamstress or her son, but her story lives with me daily because of the love and sacrifice she made for her child. Unfortunately, it made no difference in the end.

The little condominium project had been converted from an apartment building built in the 1960s, some fifteen years before I inspected it, and it was very clean and secure. The developer had renovated it with a red brick facade, covering the concrete blocks to make it look almost like a New England countryside inn. It was an ideal location for young families and retirees; the thirty-five unit, five-story building on Kewalo Street in Makiki had underground parking and was close to the bus line.

The real estate agent was waiting for me as I walked up to the building. She was in her mid-forties, medium height, trim, local Japanese, and smartly dressed in a simple, short, black dress with three wide gold chains around her neck. She was wearing the real estate agent's mandatory wristwatch, a steel and gold Oyster Perpetual Datejust Rolex, and her shoes and pocketbook matched.

"Hi! I'm Kimberly Nakamura,* agent for the seller and Mrs. Watanabe's niece."

The apartment was small, 750 square feet, with two bedrooms and one bath. It was extremely clean, and the walls, ceiling, vinyl flooring, appliances, cabinets, bathroom and kitchen fixtures were all stark white. It was so bright inside that I almost wanted to put my sunglasses on.

However, that was not what was most noticeable. In the living room there were five, three-foot tall Japanese girl dolls, each wearing a beautiful, but different, kimono. As a doll collector since childhood, I noticed the details of the work immediately. The faces were hand painted on white porcelain and the hair on each one was comprised of individual threads, intricately braided and arranged to accent the little faces perfectly. The kimonos appeared to be made from silk of a past era. The work on each one was exquisite.

"These are gorgeous." I said.

"Yes, they are, aren't they," she said, sighing deeply.

"What's the matter?"

"Nothing."

I walked around the little apartment and noticed there were no clothes in the closet and no food in the cabinets. The second bedroom was empty, with a bare twin mattress laid against a wall. The other bedroom still had Mrs. Watanabe's personal items, and the double bed was covered with bright yellow sheets. On the dresser was an old black and white photograph of a young, attractive Japanese couple. He was in his best suit, sitting stoically, staring solemnly into the camera. She was standing next to him in a beautiful Kimono, holding a bouquet of ginger and *pikake* flowers. It was her wedding picture.

"There's no clothes or food here. Did your Aunt pass away recently?"

"No, at least not yet," and with that she started crying.

"Okay, sit down. Tell me what's going on with your Aunt," I said.

Kiyoko Takiguchi* was born to indentured farmers in the Yamaguchi Prefecture in 1920, and came to Hawaii in 1940 as a picture bride. She married Kazuo Watanabe,* and in 1953, they surprised each other when, thinking they would always be childless, they produced their only child, a son, Benjamin.* Kazuo worked for Mid-Pacific Lumber Company as a lumber/sales foreman and Kiyoko became a seamstress, making custom dresses for the upper crust ladies of the Pacific and Oahu Country Clubs. Together they purchased a tiny house in Liliha, a block from the bakery where they often ate breakfast together on Sunday, their only day off.

In 1987, while playing golf on the Ala Wai Golf Course with his buddies, Kazuo suffered a fatal heart attack. After her husband's death, Kiyoko, now 67, had a hard time making ends meet, which was in large part because they had been completely supporting Ben, who at 34 years of age, was unmarried, living with them, and continuing to pursue his Jazz guitar career even though he had never performed for pay.

Kiyoko sold her home and purchased the little apartment free and clear and continued to sew for money to help Ben, but unfortunately, her eyesight began to fail because of macular degeneration, and the haute club ladies rejected her work. Still in need of an income, she started to make the Japanese dolls for sale to doll collectors. She got the kimonos from relatives in Japan and the porcelain faces in Chinatown.

As her vision continued to fail, she had her nephew, Kimberly's husband, Jim,* paint the apartment in glossy white so the light could help her see. Sewing the dresses was from memory, for the most part, and she learned to let her fingers be her eyes, and with them, would "see" the threads, braiding the fine strings into dolls' hair.

The dolls in the living room were the last ones she had made before suffering a massive stroke at the age of 83, four weeks before I came to appraise her apartment. She was now in the Intensive Care Unit at Kuakini Hospital in a drug-induced coma, with poor chance of survival.

As soon as he heard his mother was incapacitated, Ben, with her power of attorney, and as executor of her trust, drained all of her bank accounts and quick-claimed the apartment into his name. He was now selling it and had already moved to Las Vegas. He was to receive $150,000 from the sale and told his cousin, now at the age of 50, he had the means to become the music star he had always dreamed about.

When Kimberly asked him about her aunt's care and the decision to keep her on life support, he told her he had kept her on life support until all the legal matters had been cleared and now with everything done, it was up to the doctors. The costs for her care were in the hands of Medicaid and Kuakini. She was their problem now, and when she died, he told her doctor to donate her body to the Medical school. He didn't want to spend the money on a service because, as he said, he needed every dime for his career. Besides, that was what she would want for him, it was his turn to enjoy life and be free.

Kimberly finished her story saying she couldn't say anything because Ben controlled everything as trustee. She wasn't even allowed to visit her aunt in ICU without his permission.

A month after our conversation, I called Kimberly and asked if the sale had gone through and how her aunt was doing.

"Auntie Kiyoko died a week after your visit; her body went to the medical school, and the apartment closed three weeks ago. I was never allowed to visit with her before she died, but Benjamin received his money and is now as happy as a clam."

"How are you doing?" I asked.

"He let me keep the dolls. He was going to toss them. He didn't think they had any value. I kept two and gave the others to family and friends. And I kept their wedding picture."

In life there are no guarantees, and sometimes, no matter how much you love your children, there are some who believe they are entitled and are ungrateful, greedy, and only care about themselves and money.

Since Kiyoko Watanabe's death, I have appraised several homes with similar circumstances. If people confide in me about their children, I always listen, but tell them to take care of themselves first and foremost. I tell them to provide for their kids, but not to forget themselves. Life is to be enjoyed, and often parents forget this and try to do too much for their children.

Kazuo and Kiyoko were completely devoted to their son, Ben. They did everything humanly possible for him, and by doing so, destroyed any ability on his part to take care of himself. It was a lesson I would never forget.

SPEEDY AND BABY

When I go to Waianae, the *manapua* (Chinese pastries) trucks are often in the neighborhood playing their music to let everyone know they're coming. Over the past thirty years, with the development of shopping centers throughout the islands where everyone goes to pur-chase everything, the trucks are unique to the rural areas of Honolulu, where in years past, they were the regular place to buy treats. They're usually old U. S. Post Office service trucks that have been repainted and revamped. They're loaded with ice cream, candy bars, hot dogs, soda, and of course *manapua*. Seeing the trucks always takes me back to happy times of my childhood when we lived in Kaneohe.

One sunny day, as I was driving up a country road, I passed a truck driving away as children went into their houses to watch televi-sion and eat their treats. It turned out to be a very sad experience for me, and tragic for an innocent creature.

It was 4:00 p.m. in the afternoon on the Saturday before Easter. I had given up smoking my cigars and drinking scotch for Lent and was driving Mom and Dad's old 1993 Ford Escort I had inherited because I was going to Makaha and it got 36 miles to the gallon. It didn't have air-conditioning, and as I drove along the Waianae coast, passing through Nanakuli and Maili, I could feel the heat coming off the streets and into my car and I started to sweat.

My assignment was to inspect a couple of duplex houses in the back of Makaha Valley. When I arrived, there was a large open field in front of four duplex buildings, used as a parking lot for the ten-ants. I parked my car about thirty feet from the first duplex, which was a bit rundown with dry rot on the deck, old termite damage, and faded exterior paint. There was a dog tied up in front of the first house. I could see she was an old female with gray hair all over her face which had once been all black to match the rest of her fur. Her water bowl was empty, even through there was a faucet just three feet away. She was sitting in the heat because the rope she was tied to was six feet too short for her to get to the cool shadows of the mango tree next to the house, and she was crying.

I got out of the car, threw my purse over my left shoulder, and with keys in one hand and a clipboard in the other, started walking towards the dog.

"Hi Sweetheart. What's the matter? You need some water? Okay, I'll get you some."

I had taken about ten steps towards her when I heard someone stomping around the corner of the house.

"I told you. You no listen. Shut the fuck up! Shut the fuck up!"

I looked up and saw a very small, thin, angry Filipino man with a dark complexion from too many days in the sun, carrying a pistol. He turned the corner, and in a split second, shot the dog, hitting her in the torso.

She and I screamed at the same time. They say when you are in total panic, things appear to happen in slow motion, and that is what happened to me.

"Shut up!" He screamed again.

Boom! Boom! The second and third shots hit her directly in the head. After the second shot, I knew she was dead, but didn't see the third one because by now I had dropped my keys, clipboard, and purse, and was running for my life back to my car. As I got to the back end of the car, I could feel that I had wet myself, and I was thinking, "What the hell am I going to do now?" My keys were ten feet in front of my car and I was by the trunk. With the heat of the day and my overwhelming terror, sweat was pouring down my face, back, and knees.

"Help! Help! Someone call the Police!"

Now the gunman was pointing the gun in my direction and was even more irate and screaming,

"I no can sleep! Shut the fuck up! Shut up!"

"Help! Help! Please somebody help me!" I was screaming back.

By now, all the neighbors were coming out and a huge Hawaiian man, who stood about 6'4" and weighed over 300 pounds, came out to see what was going on.

As he surveyed the carnage and saw me screaming he yelled, "Speedy*, what you do? Awue! Speedy, you kill Baby! Why you do dat?"

"She no shut up. I no can sleep."

"Help!" I screamed again.

"Who you?" The huge Hawaiian asked as he looked at me and realized there was someone screaming who wasn't part of the neighborhood.

"I'm from the landlord. Call the police!"

"Landlord! Oh shit!"

He now turned and said, "Speedy, gimme me da gun."

"No fucking way," and he started to wave it in the air again.

"Speedy, no fooling now. Gimme me da gun," and with that, he stepped into Speedy's face, grabbed the pistol in one hand and virtually picked up the smaller man who desperately was not letting go of the gun. With his other hand, he hit Speedy squarely in the face, forcing him to release the pistol and knocking him to the ground.

"Junior, watch him," he said, as he tucked the gun in his pants and walked over to me.

"Sistah. What you need? You like one beer?"

"No, I need to take pictures for the landlord."

"Okay, come with me and I take you."

I picked my belongings up from the ground and walked by Speedy as he sat holding his face and whimpering.

"Sistah, you sure you sure you no like one beer?"

"No, really, I'm good, but we should call the police."

"No way, Sistah, we need Speedy. He gets our stuffs faster than Pizza Hut delivers."

"So what, he's tweaking now?" I said.

"Yeah. Da Kine, so stupid. He likes his stuffs too and no make money because it all goes up his nose or in his pipe."

I took my pictures of the units, thanked him, and as I drove off, everyone waved and smiled. No one seemed concerned and I sensed this was probably because it was just a typical day in the valley. I called my brother, Steven, on my cell phone and told him about Speedy and Baby.

"Come to Shokudo, we'll buy you dinner."

On the drive home, I found one of my cigars in the glove compartment and lit up. I knew God would understand my early breaking of the Lenten fast. I smoked it all the way back to Honolulu. When I got to the restaurant, I ordered a double Scotch, and with two hands firmly on the glass, drank it down in less then three minutes. With the warmth of the liquor flowing through my veins, I retold the story over dinner to my brother, his wife, and a mutual friend; no one said anything. Steven just shook his head from time to time. When we finished eating, I was reluctant to leave them, and I guess it was obvious.

"You okay to drive home? Want us to follow you?"

"No, I'm good."

When I got home, I had another two drinks as it was now Easter morning, then fell into bed for a long, deep sleep.

I called the landlord on Monday morning and told him what had happened, but he had already heard about Speedy and Baby. He said no one had done anything about her body and she lay in the searing sun all day before Speedy sobered up and buried her, but by then, the smell had hit all the neighbors and they complained to him.

He had been planning to evict the entire group down the line, but now, with the past weekend's shooting, he was sending out the termination notices in the coming week.

"Don't need drug dealers or users on my property," he said.

To this day, every time I go to the Waianae Coast, I smile when I observe the *manapua* trucks rambling down the roads, but when I see them I also always remember to say a prayer for that old dog, Baby. The landlord told me Speedy had been so high for three days before he shot her, that he forgot to feed or water her all that time. She was crying because she was so hungry and thirsty. None of the thirty or so people living in the complex helped her because they themselves were either higher than kites like Speedy, or just didn't want to be bothered.

KAREN ERTELL

She was a petite, yet sturdy blond Caucasian, dressed in a short, blue sundress and rubber flip-flops. I could tell she was very determined as she walked into the modest little warehouse in Kakaako, behind the Ward Theatres to inspect the coffee-roasting business another broker and I were selling together in 2003.

My clients were calling me the "Coffee Queen," as I had bought and sold eight coffee businesses during the heyday of the coffee craze of the late 1990s and early 2000s, and this was the last one of them. In those days, it was almost everyone's dream to own a coffee house or kiosk, hoping to reap the rewards from the aroma of Colombian or Kona coffee beans wafting through the air of crowded malls and street corners.

Karen Ertell had never been in the coffee-roasting business before, but at this point in her life, she wanted to try something different.

"It's a lot of hard work, and Starbucks is coming in everywhere. You'll have to work long hours and build a niche for yourself. I always tell people who have never owned a business before that they'll have to be married to it for many years." I said.

"I know, and I already have ideas of how to grow the business," she said to me with great conviction.

A deal was made; she set her goals, revamped, and increased the efficiency of the roasting process, and as a result, grew her market position with a steady stream of customers. I would see her from time to time at the Kapiolani Community College farmers' market where she had a retail spot every Saturday morning. She started out alone, but over time, she hired staff, and her clientele continued to increase as larger coffee houses and restaurants wanted her Hawaiian roasted beans. In 2006, *Honolulu* magazine named her company the best local coffee-roaster in Hawaii.

In August, 2005, I was assigned to do a refinancing appraisal for Karen. She had purchased a house through a foreclosure just before the real estate market exploded and prices soared. After making some improvements, she was ready to lower her interest rate and pull out some dollars to put back into her home and business.

The house was on Akua Street, and according to the *Hawaiian Dictionary*, *Akua* in Hawaiian principally means God. However, it has lesser meanings, such as spirit, ghost, devil, corpse, or supernatural.

As I drove up I could see the neighborhood was old and rundown. There were no sidewalks, and a couple of broken-down, rusted-out cars sat on the road a little beyond her house. Her neighbors' yards were over-grown, there was loose garbage on the streets, and many of the houses were badly in need of renovation.

Karen's house, built during the 1950s, was of simple, single-wall construction, and in need of painting. However, as I walked into her home, I saw it was clean and well-maintained. There was a warm feeling throughout and this atmosphere was reinforced when her two sloppy- tongued, happy dogs greeted me and escorted me all over the house. She loved Elvis Presley and had a life size cutout of him in one of her bedrooms. She said she liked the company.

A upright piano, a recent purchase, was just off the living room and as I was looking at it, she confided in me, "I decided to learn how to play before I was fifty, which will be in a year."

"I just did the same thing! I'm learning through internet lessons," I said.

"You need a real teacher. You can't learn well without someone pushing you."

While I was sitting in the living room, dogs at my feet, and drawing the dimensions of the house, I asked her to play something for me. She played a classical piece beautifully and I looked at her and said,

"You're right. I do need a human teacher. You are much more advanced than I."

She nodded and smiled, pleased with the complement.

As she walked me out to my car, I turned to her and said, "Karen, this area of Ewa Beach is pretty rundown and a bit seedy. I've heard there are some gang and drug activities around here. It's not a safe neighborhood for a small, single girl like you. Are you sure you want to stay here? You could sell this house, make a profit, and flip into a better neighborhood."

She looked straight into my eyes, and with great conviction said, "I love my neighbors. They're good to me. They always look out for me and protect me."

On May 27, 2007, while watching the evening news, I learned Karen Ertell had been murdered in her own home. Captain Frank

Fujii of the Honolulu Police Department, described her murder in the May 28, 2007, issue of the *Honolulu Star Bulletin*, as "outrageously heinous in the nature of the crime."

Within four days of the murder, police arrested Karen's neighbor, Vernon Bartley. He was fifteen years old and had been a troubled youth in his native New Zealand before coming to Hawaii. Bartley had been a chronic problem for Karen over the past year by continually breaking into her home and stealing her possessions. She had caught him several times and made him pay her back by cleaning her yard. When he didn't stop his malevolent deeds, she decided to testify against him in court over his thievery so that he would get the professional help she believed he needed to turn his life around.

Within days of her death, Bartley confessed to the crimes against Karen. He had strangled her from behind and had sex with her, although the medical examiner could not determine whether she was alive or dead at the time. When he was finished with Karen, and she lay dead in the back bedroom, he hung around the house for hours and used her computer to watch pornography. He then took her money, credit cards, and Volvo out joy riding and met up with friends.

Vernon Bartley was convicted of murder and received a life sentence plus ten years with the possibility of parole. This was because the judge believed, at his young age there was a chance for rehabilitation. The court gave him a future down the road, but sadly, there was none for Karen.

When I think of Karen Ertell, I'm haunted by the last words she spoke to me. She was a very confident person who believed in the goodness and decency of people, especially her neighbors. She thought they would protect her at all times, but instead, they failed her in her greatest hour of need. They betrayed her by not having the integrity to stand up to a young man who became a monster. He needed help and guidance long before he ever met Karen, but everyone was afraid to speak out or take action.

THE BUBBLEHEAD

It was five o'clock sharp on a Friday afternoon when I arrived at the house in Village Park, Ewa. The tenant selected the time because he said he had to work until then.

When I walked up to the door and met him, something inside told me he was trouble, and my feelings were confirmed as soon as I entered the house. The front door had a dead bolt that locked with a key from either the front or the back. After we entered, he turned and locked the door and placed the key in his front right pocket. The entire house was very dark because black out curtains covered all the windows, with the exception of the kitchen and a couple of windows in the living room.

The tenant, Mr. T,* was about thirty years old, tall and trim. He had dirty blond hair, cut short, wore black, horn-rimmed glasses, and was dressed in blue jeans and a white tee shirt. I thought he looked a bit like mass-murderer Jeffery Dahmer.

"I see you're not wearing a ring. Are you married?"

"No, I'm not. Are you?" I asked.

"No, but my wife is," he said with an evil grin. "She's gone for awhile, visiting her mother, I think." he continued, "So would you be interested in a little play time?"

I looked at him, frowned, and ignored his question. This seemed to agitate him. He began to tense his arms and rub his hands. As I walked around the house, he followed closely, about two or three feet away. When I went into the dining room, I almost jumped out of my skin. There was no dining furniture; instead, he had a queen-size bed where the table should have been, and it was covered with soiled, black and red satin sheets. The walls were painted solid black.

As he continued to follow me around, he didn't say much of anything, but just stared, and I felt as though his piercing glare went right through me.

We ended up in the kitchen, and with the light, I noticed his eyes for the first time; they were very cloudy and he was sniffing a lot. As I started drawing the dimensions of the house on the kitchen countertop, I saw him, from the corner of my eye, pull out a large carving knife from a wood block. He turned to face me, and then started to look at the knife. With it, he started to clean his nails, one by one.

He looked up after a few moments and said, "No one knows you're here, do they?"

"My office knows where I am at all times. I give them my itinerary." I said.

"Yes, but it's the weekend and after five now and everyone has gone home," he said as he looked intently at me, continuing to clean his nails.

I could feel the back of my hair stand up and my gut was screaming at me to get out, but the front door was locked and the key was in his pocket. I looked around the kitchen, trying not to show the fear that was quickly consuming me. Behind him, I could see the back door to the carport. It didn't have a dead bolt, but he was between the door and me.

I backed up a few steps, with sketchpad and pen in my hands, acting as if I was looking at the house to complete my illustration. With the knife still in his hands, he continued to stare and smile at me. Then, as I looked around, I saw the pictures hanging in a small alcove for the first time.

"You're a Bubblehead! Wow! Your father must be so proud!"

"What?" He said.

You're a submariner. My Dad was in the Navy too! He told me about you Bubbleheads. To become a submariner you must go through rigorous tests, and the final exam has you going from one end of the ship to the other blindfolded to get to your duty station and perform your tasks. Your Dad must think you are the greatest."

"My Dad? Yes, yes, he is very proud." He stammered.

He put the knife down on the countertop and came toward me to look at the pictures of his submarine, him and his buddies in uniform, as well as his citations.

"Wow, a Navy and Marine medal! A Good Conduct medal! You're a hero. Your father must talk about you constantly."

"Yes, yes, my Dad is very proud." His eyes looked liked they were starting to clear as he focused on the pictures.

"Wow, look at all you guys on deck with your medals. Heroes, every one of you!" I practically shouted.

As he looked at the photographs, intently trying to see what I was seeing, I slowly and quietly backed up into the kitchen.

"If I was your Mom, with all your medals, I'd be proud of you too."

He was now fixed on the citations and didn't notice me stealthily slinking into the kitchen.

Then I made my move. Backing up a few more steps, in one complete turn, I unlocked the back door and opened it.

"Thank you, Mr. T. I have everything I need now. Thank you for your hospitality. Goodbye." And I was out the door.

I ran to my car, jumped in and locked the door. I was shaking and sweating. He didn't follow me, and in a few moments I was back on the road, on my way home. Driving through the neighborhood,

I realized no one was in the houses around Mr. T's house. It is a working-class neighborhood and I suspected everyone was in transit to or from work.

I don't know what would have happened that afternoon if I had not seen the photographs and known about submariners, but the sinister atmosphere of the experience changed how I do business. Nowadays I never schedule appointments in the late afternoon. When I do have meetings, I always get together with people in open, well-traveled, areas.

For showings or inspections, the appointments are set between 10:00 a.m. and 2:00 p.m. because most people are alert and sober during this time. More importantly, there are other people working in and around the vicinity.

I also started wearing a ring on my left hand when I go on inspections. The ring looks like a wedding band and most times, when people see it, they assume that I'm married, which is fine with me. It stops a lot of "do you want to play" conversations, particularly in places you don't want to have these dialogues. Now, I always carry a telephone, and let someone know where I am at all times.

These situations have made me more aware of people's behavior. In the business of real estate, we are always meeting individuals we haven't met before...at homes, warehouses, industrial areas, and open acreage. Many times, in these circumstances, there is no one around to hear you scream if trouble comes.

All my senses told me I was in big trouble that day in the late afternoon when I first arrived at Mr. T's house. I initially chose to disregard those feelings, but lucky for me, my gut kept shrieking at me until I listened to it. This was another lesson I learned; if your inner voice tells you there is something wrong, listen to it, don't ignore your intuition. Get out of the situation immediately.

MOLOKAI MAN

Kalani Hoku* or "Molokai Man," as I call him, was a big athletic, nineteen-year-old when his car hit black ice on his way home from a party and slammed into a semi-truck on a California highway. Originally from the island of Molokai, Kalani was not familiar with mainland weather, and when he recovered from the accident many months later, he was a quadriplegic.

When you first meet Kalani, his handsome face and tremendous charisma are the first things you notice about him, and not that he is in a wheelchair.

"Ms. Sofos, I need an appraisal for a foreclosure property I'm buying on Molokai, and I heard you're the person who can do it for me," he said, as he extended his hand to shake mine when we first met.

We chatted for several minutes, and then I said, "There are no addresses posted on Molokai…everyone just tells me it's the third house on the left after the telephone pole. Or something like that. How will I find it?" I asked.

"My brother-in-law will meet you at the airport and drive you to the property."

Since I hadn't been to Molokai in a couple of years, I thought it would be a fun day-trip to see the island again so I agreed to do it.

When I landed at the tiny terminal in Kaunakakai, it was hot and humid, and I was already in a sticky sweat. Kalani's brother-in-law, Sam*, was there in his tiny, white, two-door Toyota Tercel, with his two-year-old child in tow. There was no air-conditioning and the youngster screamed from the moment I got into the car until I left the island five hours later.

"So have you seen the property?" I asked.

"Yes".

"Is it nice?"

"It's okay."

He was not much for conversation, and after a half hour of driving, we arrived at the property. He parked on the side of the road and we got out.

"You need to walk in from here," he pointed as he gave me a set of keys to the house.

"Why don't we just drive up to the house?" I asked him.

"The family is upset about the foreclosure and I don't want to offend them as I also live nearby."

"Okay, no problem," I said as I walked towards the house. Much of the west side of Molokai is parched and water has always been an issue for the land. However, as I walked into the property, I could see it was located in a very lush area, almost like a rainforest in the midst of a desert. The house was on a long, rectangular, one-acre lot, in the middle of a large mango grove. It was so thick with trees and shrubbery I had to take my sunglasses off so my eyes could adjust and I could see where I was walking. About 150 feet inward, I saw the house, and adjacent to it about thirty feet away, was a large camper's tent. A tall, muscular, young Hawaiian man with long, flowing black hair stood up as I approached. He was barefooted and clad in a tank top and board shorts and was kneeling next to a small campfire cooking a meal. Turning slightly towards the tent, he said something inaudible, all the while keeping his eyes fixed on me. Soon a young, equally fit Hawaiian woman came out of the tent. She was carrying what looked like a 30-30 Winchester rifle and handed it to the young man.

"Ka-chook!" I clearly heard the distinct sound of the cocking of the rifle.

I had walked past them, but now stopped dead in my tracks and turned towards them; we were now facing each other about twenty feet away. While they were not pointing the rifle directly at me, but more in my vicinity, they were clearly staring me down, and their message was obvious.

After fifteen seconds of this, and weighing my options, I looked right at them and met their intense gazes.

"Look, you know I'm here because of the court order. I'm truly sorry about the situation, but I have a job to do. If you don't let me do my inspection, then I, or someone else will be back with the sheriff and things will just get worse. I'm going to walk around the property and through the house, and I won't disturb anything. I'm going to start walking now."

I turned my back on them and started walking toward the back of the property. Sweat was pouring off my face and I was afraid my knees would buckle.

"Ka-chook!"

I heard it again, but this time I did not turn around or flinch; I just kept walking. I opened up the house with shaking hands, walked in and locked the door behind me. They didn't come after me, and I completed my inspection. When I walked back to the car I exited on the opposite side of the property to avoid the campers. My hands were still shaking and my shirt was completely soaked.

"Did you know they would be there? And that they would be armed?" I asked Sam.

"Yes and yes."

"And the reason you didn't tell me, was what?" I pressed, as anger started to set in.

"Well, because if I said anything, then you probably wouldn't have gone in and done the work and Kalani needs the report like yesterday. Now we're done so let's go eat!" After a quick lunch at Dairy Queen, he took me on a tour of the entire island all the while telling me tales of the island's people and families to calm me down before bringing me back to the airport.

When I got back to Honolulu, I called Kalani, but before I could say anything, he said, "I heard and I'm really sorry for the trouble. I knew they wouldn't hurt you, but only try to scare you."

"Well they succeeded." I said.

He chuckled a bit and said, "I heard you don't scare easy, Ms. Sofos, and that's why I asked you to help me. And, Ms. Sofos, I really want thank you so much for your help. I really appreciate it." I could hear the smile in his voice.

There was no sense in telling him I had been terrified out of my mind and was thinking of strangling him the next time I saw him. He sounded so sincere that I believed him.

Over the years, I've learned much about Kalani. His doctors consider him a medical miracle because he has gained the reuse of his arms and hands with hard work and sheer willpower. He still has pain throughout his body every day, which makes him feel like he's on fire, but he goes on without pain medication. If something seems impossible, he figures it out. He will not ask for help unless he truly needs it, because he is determined to be independent, even with his handicap. Today, Kalani is a successful, mini real-estate mogul as he continues to buy dilapidated properties, fix them up, and rent them.

Kalani's life, and who he has become, have been a true inspiration, and yet another lesson for me. He is a straightforward and genuine person who faces adversity everyday of his life, but doesn't give up or give in. I often try to emulate Molokai man as he will forever be one of my greatest heroes.

CHAPTER TWENTY-NINE

Politics And Business Come Together

"Hello. Is this Stephany Sofos?"

"Yes."

"This is Mildred Mizuno* of the governor's Office."

"Which governor?"

"Miss Sofos, this is Governor Cayetano's office calling."

"Yeah, right."

"Miss Sofos, Governor Cayetano would like you to come for breakfast at Washington Place this Thursday at 8 a.m. Can you make it?"

"Come on, who are you, someone from a radio 'gotcha' show? I laughed.

"Miss Sofos, This is the governor's office and I need your response, please." I could tell she was clearly upset with me. Could she really be from the governor's office? "Okay, I'll bite, why would the governor want to see me?"

"He wants to talk to you about the report you wrote that appeared in last week's *Honolulu Advertiser*."

In June, 1997, I did a cost analysis for a dozen small retail businesses in Honolulu. I was so shocked at the impact of what I termed our "Paradise Tax," or the overall financial burdens of shipping, delivery, excise taxes, and mandatory health care requirements for employees, that I released some of the information to the *Honolulu Advertiser*. I discovered that even if a local business did well with high gross sales, they could not compete with mainland U.S. and international retailers here in Hawaii. No matter how hard they tried, the best they could do was to break even or make a small profit.

The bigger the merchants, the larger the discounts they receive on merchandise, shipping, and even rents, because of their immense volume. These mainland-owned behemoths were able to obtain cheaper health care packages, advertising, uniforms, supplies, etc. through their mainland subsidiaries. The cost of living in Hawaii was about thirty-five percent higher than the mainland U.S., and in today's world, that percentage is probably a lot higher.

On Thursday at 7:45 a.m. I drove to the back gate of Washington Place. After a security check, I was told to park in the back and walk to the front of the mansion. The grounds remained much as they had been when Queen Liliuokalani lived there more than a century before, with their lush gardens and large shade trees, and as I passed the tennis court, I reminisced about my days at the Priory when we were allowed to play on the governor's tennis court since the school is the mansion's next-door neighbor.

Before I could even knock, the door opened and a maid in full uniform greeted me and walked me into the large living room. I sat down on the couch, and within five minutes the governor came downstairs from his private living quarters. He was, as always, impeccably dressed in a light gray Italian suit, polished black shoes, and neatly combed hair. We introduced ourselves and I gave him a few cigars from my dad, as I knew he smoked them occasionally while playing golf.

Governor Cayetano, for all his bravado, is actually a bit shy, and when we met he was somewhat at a loss for words. After a few moments, while waiting for the First Lady, he asked if we had met before. "Yes, we met a couple of times at the Honolulu Club," I said. This small connection helped establish an instant affinity.

Vicky, the First Lady, soon appeared at the foot of stairs and together they escorted me into the formal dining room where Elizabeth II, Emperor Hirohito of Japan, past U.S. presidents, and the last queen of Hawaii, whose portrait dominated the room, had once dined.

Over papaya and French toast we talked for over two hours about the state of Hawaii's economy and the "Paradise Tax." During the course of our chat, assistants came into the room and politely reminded the governor he would be late for a couple of meetings. He waved them off and told them to reschedule them for later in the day, as he wanted to continue our dialogue.

Like the determined litigator he was before entering politics, his questions to me were sharp and to the point, and if he was unfamiliar with a technical term, he rephrased the question so that he clearly understood the answer. Before we parted, the Governor and First Lady took me for a quick tour of the mansion's downstairs. When I left, he said he would be talking with me again soon.

Two weeks after our breakfast, I received a call from the Deputy Director of the State of Hawaii's Department of Business, Economic

Development, and Tourism. "Ms. Sofos, this is William Walker* of DBEDT. The governor asked me to convey his invitation to you to be on his Economic Revitalization Task Force."

"What is it?" I asked.

"The Governor is bringing key private and public sector people together to come up with ideas to move our state forward in these difficult economic times."

"I'll have to think about it and get back to you." I said. Three days later, Mr. Walker called again. "Ms. Sofos, the governor wants you on the Task Force."

"Well, how much time will it take? I don't get a salary and time and income are the same to me," I said.

Clearly frustrated, his voice now terse, he said, "Ms. Sofos, the biggest leaders of the state will be on this Task Force and the governor has made it very clear to me that he wants you to be a part of it. It shouldn't take more then a few days of your time.

"Okay, okay. I'll do it," I reluctantly agreed.

Hawaii in 1997 was at an economic and political crossroads; the economy was failing and seemed to have been bypassed by the rest of the nation in economic prosperity. Tourism, now our only really profitable industry, was in the doldrums; everyone could see if something wasn't done soon, the situation would worsen for the state and the democratic party, which had ruled Hawaii for over thirty-five years. After much discussion, the governor, senate president, and speaker of the house agreed to put together a task force of members of the private and public sectors. Their goal was to come up with new ideas on restructuring government in order to revitalize the state and get it moving again.

The Task Force was comprised of twenty-six members:

Governor Cayetano, Senate President Norman Mizuguchi, Speaker of the House Joe Souki and retired Judge Walter Heen, all of whom represented the state government. Gary Rodrigues, director of the United Public Workers Union, Russell Okata, director of the Hawaii Government Employees Association, and Bruce Coppa, director of Pacific Resource Partnership, represented the unions.

Walter Dods, chairman of First Hawaiian Bank, and Larry Johnson, chairman of Bank of Hawaii, represented the big banks. Richard Kelley, Chairman of Outrigger Enterprises, Stanley Takahashi, Chief Operating Officer of Kyo-Ya Co. Ltd., and Roy Tokujo, CEO of Cove Marketing were there for the hotels and tourism industry. Doc Byers, CEO of C. Brewer, John Couch, Chairman of Alexander & Baldwin, and Charlie King, represented the last of the Big Five corporations and old missionary landed gentry, who until the 1960s, had ruled Hawaii for over 100 years and still owned tens of thousands of acres of land in Hawaii.

Bob Clarke, CEO of Hawaiian Electric Company, Larry Fuller, Publisher of the *Honolulu Advertiser*, John Reed, president of Duty Free Services, and Stanley Hong, CEO of the Chamber of Commerce of Hawaii, represented other big businesses. Chad Wright, president of Hawaii Pacific University, and Ken Mortimer, president of the University of Hawaii were there for education.

Barry Taniguchi, CEO of KTA Super Stores, Diana Plotts, chairman of Hawaii Health Systems, Corp., Don Malcolm, Patricia Loui, president of Omnitrak Group, and I represented small business.

When I walked into the first meeting, I realized mine was the smallest business by far, as I am a sole proprietor. I have no secretaries, no assistants, no staff, nothing... as I prefer to outsource everything.

Our first meeting in July was in one of Bank of Hawaii's meeting rooms and when I showed up hardly anyone knew who I was or why I was there. They were all rather standoffish and pretty much ignored me, with the exception of the governor who greeted me with a bear hug and kiss and said, "Thank you for being here."

Tom Leppert, Vice Chairman of Bank of Hawaii, and who would go on to become mayor of Dallas, Texas, was the facilitator and moderator. He started the meeting by stating that Hawaii must recognize that the world has changed, and if we are to compete, we must change too.

Tom went on to say, "You need to be bold and fly at 30,000 feet and not get caught up in the micromanagement of the issues. You need to focus on the overall goals and benefits for all of us in Hawaii."

Discussion followed, and when the issue of tourism came up, Doc Byers commented, "We were a beautiful lady to whom men came calling from 1959 to 1993, but we're no longer the beautiful lady and we're having to compete more, especially in Waikiki."

Disliking sexism, I piped up, "Well, we could also say Waikiki was a handsome young man who grew old and became bald and fat." Everyone chuckled with the exception of Doc, probably because he was older, bald, and a bit overweight.

After about an hour of discussion, I decided I had nothing to lose by adding my two cents. "Mr. Leppert, may I make a comment?"

"Yes, Ms. Sofos."

"We need specific goals to present to the public by our October deadline. A lot of people think this is smoke and mirrors. They think people in power don't want change because they like the status quo and they are making money. If you don't tell the legislature specific things, people are not going to believe you."

No one said a word for about five seconds; the silence was deafening. Finally, the governor spoke and said, "She's right. Let's make sure we are specific."

From that moment on, I was validated and regarded as someone of substance in the group. Walter Dods and Larry Johnson came over to me at our next break and both told me that my comment was excellent and the step that needed to be taken to get change for Hawaii.

Over the next several months, the members split up and met in small focus groups to get their ideas organized on how to reinvent and revitalize Hawaii. In October, the Task Force convened at the JAIMS (Japan-American Institute of Management Science) training center in Hawaii Kai for two days, meeting from eight in the morning to ten at night. When we finished, our entire group, coming from so many different directions and ideologies, unanimously approved our package of recommendations.

Our proposals were straightforward and uncomplicated; cut income and business taxes up to fifty percent, which had never been done before. Increase the gross excise tax, giving certain industries exemptions so as not to kill their businesses. This would stimulate the economy and put more dollars in the pockets of individuals and companies. Everyone believed this would balance the state's revenue stream with an increase on a tax that would put most of the burden on tourists.

Other proposals were to eliminate government red tape on land issues, improve government services, make the University of Hawaii world class by giving it autonomy, improve our public school system by establishing county-based, appointed school boards, and increase the hotel room tax. Finally, a tourism advisory board would be set up to oversee the expenditure of additional funding raised for advertising and promotion of this vital industry.

To me it seemed so simple, but when we were asked by the governor to go out to the public to explain it, I was unprepared for the hostility that awaited us. The hate mail began almost immediately, as well as the personal insults and public comments about our intelligence and allegiance. On Kauai, a young, longhaired, environmentalist called me a pig to my face and told me that I was "avaricious and nefarious." In Moiliili, I was told I was a "lackey for the Governor".

Certain politicians were against the recommendations because some of their pet projects would be phased out with the cuts in income taxes. A senator on the legislature's ways and means committee said to me, "I don't want to support cuts. If I had my way, all you people would pay ninety percent of your income to taxes. You're loaded and can afford it."

"I am not loaded." I responded. "I have good years and bad years. I've been close to bankruptcy twice in the last five years. I don't get a pension. This is about equity, I said.

"I don't give a rat's ass about equity," he hissed. "I only care about the dollars I can get for my constituents. They are poor, and we, as government, need to feed them and give them homes."

"You won't have money to feed anyone if you don't help business," I replied.

"Business will survive, no matter how much we squeeze them. It's the nature of the beast. You all will find a way to make money."

One city councilman, who would later become a mayoral candidate for Honolulu, even said to me, "Why should I support these proposals? I should have been named to the task force because I'm in charge of the city's finances as the council's budget committee's chairman. Why were you picked and what could you possibly bring to the table?"

Eventually, most of what we suggested was passed by the legislature over the next three years. Income and business taxes were cut, the excise tax was not increased, the University of Hawaii received its autonomy, the hotel room tax was increased, and a Tourism Authority was created. As a result, individuals and businesses grew robustly and Hawaii, for the next ten years, experienced some of its most productive years.

I believe that what Governor Cayetano and members of the task force accomplished was truly visionary. However, in retrospect, I realize I was quite naïve back then because I sincerely believed the increase in taxes, particularly the gross excise tax, was going for a greater good.

Unfortunately, over the years I have seen that no matter how much our taxes are increased, it will never be enough for some of the small-minded politicians who control our existence, because while there are a few who want to help the downtrodden, as in the John Kennedy ideology, there are many more who simply want to manipulate the community for their own ambitions. They hunger to grab as much money as can be squeezed out of the public for their personal legacy projects.

If the task force were assembled today, the package of recommendations to grow the economy would not have had unanimous approval. I now would never agree to any type of increase in revenue enhancements for government.

CHAPTER THIRTY

Carpetbaggers And Scalawags

It all started with Kamehameha the Great. After conquering and uniting the islands (with the exception of Kauai, Niihau and Kahoolawe) he quickly discerned that Naval vessels and whalers from all over the world coveted his bays and harbors because of their strategic location, particularly as an ideal place to replenish their food supplies. He allowed the ships access to Lahaina, Kealakekua, Hilo, and Honolulu for hefty fees. He even moved his home from Waikiki to downtown Honolulu, where the present Harbor Court condominium stands, just to make sure that the ships paid their duties and to keep watch over activities. In a relatively short period of time, by western standards, he became quite wealthy.

Barely a year after his death in 1819, American Congregational missionaries from Boston arrived in Hawaii to spread the word of

God among the natives, whose ancient religious system had been abandoned after the death of the great chief. "God's People," as they were often called, quickly saw the potential of Hawaii, and as the old story goes, "they came to do good, and did very well." Their descendants, with their western education, took over important posts in the kingdom and were rewarded with much acreage from royal land grants.

In 1843, an illegal five-month British occupation took place in Hawaii because of a land dispute between the king and the British Consul. Admiral Richard Thomas (after whom Thomas Square in Honolulu is named) Commander of the British Squadron in the Pacific, under direct orders from Queen Victoria, restored the kingdom's sovereignty to Kamehameha III, and on July 31, 1843, His Royal Highness created the motto, "Ua Mau Ke Ea O Ka Aina I Ka Pono," which translated, means, "The Life of the Land is Perpetuated in Righteousness." These words, uttered on the steps of Kawaiahao Church, became the motto of the kingdom.

Until 1848 the king owned all the land throughout the islands. Kamehameha III came under increasing pressure from foreign sources, as well as non-Hawaiian citizens of the kingdom, to abolish the ancient feudal land system. This eventually led to the Great Mahele of 1848 which called for the redistribution of all the land between the government, king, chiefs, and commoners, and allowed fee simple ownership of land in the islands for the first time.

Despite the division of land that resulted from the Great Mahele, a large portion of land in Hawaii continues to be owned by large estates. Most of them were established by the *alii* (chiefs) of the Hawaiian Kingdom. The largest was, and still is, Bishop Estate/Kamehameha Schools who at one time owned 336,373 acres of land, or about 10%. of the land on all the islands. Other large landowners are the estates of Queen Emma and Queen Liliuokalani, both of which hold title to many valuable pieces of real estate, mostly in Waikiki.

On the windward side of the island, Kaneohe Ranch, which was founded by Harold K.L. Castle and who was a missionary descendent owned much of the land. On the Ewa plains, James Campbell's estate owned over 80,000 acres until it was dissolved in 2008 and the assets passed on to 31 living heirs.

While these large trusts controlled the land, the "Big Five," a group of large corporations, some of which were founded also by missionary descendents, controlled the economy. They were: Castle & Cooke, Alexander and Baldwin, C. Brewer & Company, American Factors, and Theo, H. Davies. Until recent years, sugar and pineapple were the major industries in Hawaii and the five companies either owned or were agents for the plantations, the mills and cannery. Alexander & Baldwin owned Matson Lines, the major shipping company in Hawaii and the sole provider of transportation for both people and goods for many years. Most other large businesses, including The Liberty House, formerly Honolulu's largest department store, was a subsidiary of American Factors until it was purchased by Macy's.

Since World War II and Statehood, although they are still some of Hawaii's largest companies, their monopoly on commerce, development, shipping, and politics no longer exists.

When King Kalakaua, the second elected monarch of the Hawaiian kingdom, came to the throne in 1874, he took advantage of his power by spending government money frivolously, much to the disdain of government leaders and businessmen. After several years of talking to an unheeding monarch, these officials and capitalists took matters into their own hands. They forced a new constitution on the king which greatly limited his powers and turned the country into a constitutional monarchy, much like that of Great Britain. This document, which the king reluctantly signed, was called the Bayonet Constitution because of the coercion put upon Kalakaua to accept it. After his death, when his sister and successor, Queen Liliuokalani, attempted to restore the former constitution and regain control of the government, she was deposed on January 17, 1893.

Hawaii then became a provincial government followed by a republic. In 1898, the islands were annexed to the United States as a territory. By the time of Liliuokalani's death in 1917, Hawaii was a valuable asset of the United States' in its efforts to become a major power in the Pacific.

The bombing of Pearl Harbor on December 7, 1941, established the importance of Hawaii's strategic location in the Pacific. In my opinion, it also impressed on the psyche of the entire nation, the desire to never let it go. When both World War II and the Korean War were over, and America was in the process of converting to a post-war economy, Hawaii took its place as the fiftieth state on May 1, 1959.

After the war, many former military families, like my parents, decided to remain in the islands because they had fallen in love with its beauty and gentle ways. When statehood was proposed, many locals, including Mom and Dad, were against it because they feared it would bring in carpetbaggers and scalawags who would take over island politics and commercialize paradise. However, there were many more islanders in favor of statehood, believing it would give them more opportunity, freedom, and a chance for advancement into the higher echelons of wealth and power.

With statehood established, as had been predicted, business and travel exploded, and outsiders throughout the other existing forty-nine states, looking for a fast buck, poured into the islands. By the

early 1960's development was taking place on all islands, old plantation towns were expanding and new cities were forming everywhere.

With this growth, others from all over the world now came in
waves, like the ebb and flow of ocean tides, hoping to own their own
piece of paradise. In the early sixties there was a huge flow of Canadi-
ans purchasing properties in the islands to escape their bitter winters.
In the early 1970's, the Middle Easterners, particularly Saudis came,
and bought much of old Kahala with their new found oil wealth.
In the late seventies, Samoans and Tongans came looking for work,
education, and land. In the early eighties, it was Koreans.

In the late 1980's and early 1990's the Japanese nationals entered
the market. Flushed with manufacturing wealth, they drove around
the neighborhoods in chauffeured limousines with suitcases full of
cash, knocking on doors, offering to buy homes they had never even
walked into. A single investor purchased over one hundred homes in
Hawaii Kai alone during this period. Their desire for Hawaiian real
estate was insatiable, and before the buying spree was over, they had
purchased most of the hotels, shopping centers, office buildings, and
farms in the islands.

With the Japanese invasion, as many called it, often using the
phrase, "They couldn't bomb us out, so they bought us out," there
was a shift in how Hawaiian real estate was thought of by both locals
and outsiders alike. Prior to this foray, most individuals viewed their
property as their home, whether primary or secondary. It was considered their own piece of heaven; now it was all about buying and
selling for a profit.

The business of Hawaiian real estate exploded and everyone from
schoolteachers, to waiters, to plumbers, got real estate licenses to
sell, sell, sell. At one point, there were almost 28,000 people with
licenses, or about one in thirty-five residents, out of a population of

one million. Some were inactive, a lot were part-timers, but most were actively looking for the opportunity to make a deal. Many foreign nationals came into the business, buying and selling for their own people. There was frenzy in the marketplace never seen before, and neighborhoods were changing drastically, particularly in east Oahu, the favorite area of the Asian market.

Older, quaint, architecturally unique homes were being torn down daily, replaced with large, concrete, centrally air-conditioned "McMansions," structures which took almost the entire land foot-print and left very little open area for outside activities. So much for the "Hawaiian sense of place," as local politicians at the time touted these new investments in Hawaii.

In 1999, the Glass-Steagall Law of 1933, which separated commercial and investment banks and helped to regulate the financial markets, was repealed under President Bill Clinton. With the federal government's assistance, money for home loans started to flood the real estate market from all directions. However, with the catastrophic destruction of the World Trade Center on September 11, 2001, everything came to a screeching halt. President George W. Bush came out the following year and told Americans it was their duty as citizens to spend and get the country moving again.

Hawaii was slow at first to embrace the new mortgage money, but then two things happened to get the islands moving again: mortgage brokers and Oprah.

When people speak about "The Oprah Effect", they aren't kidding. Her power to influence public opinion in areas of book sales, elections, and even food markets, has been well documented, and it found its way into Hawaii real estate.

In 2003, Oprah and Donald Trump were chatting on her show about investing in real estate and both of them agreed that Hawaii and specifically, the east side of the island of Hawaii, in the Hilo and Puna districts, were the up-and-coming areas to own. With land prices from lows of $1,000 to highs of $30,000 per acre, the ability to purchase paradise was within the grasp of most Americans.

Within days after that show, Big Island real estate agents were flooded with inquiries about homes and land in the Hawaiian Acres, Hawaiian Beaches, Pahoa, Kapoho, and Kalapana sub-divisions. This new awareness spread not only in America, but around the world, and there was sudden global interest in Hawaiian real estate once again.

Many real estate agents, who had not made much money since 9-11, jumped into the mortgage business and became mortgage solicitors. Back then, to become a solicitor required only purchase of a license and a broker to hang it with, and then they could assist clients to buy, as well as finance, property.

Also, a lot of real estate agents and mortgage brokers fueled the frenzy by buying and selling properties for themselves. They could see the latest houses coming to market before the general public because of their access to the multiple listing service, and would jump on the properties and place them in escrow right away. With their connections to the sub-prime lenders, they often had access to houses before closing and were able to cosmetically fix them. These agents would then "flip" the properties for a substantial profit and double commissions in what's called "back-to-back closings" in the industry. That is, selling to another client before escrow closes and their initial purchase has been funded.

From 2003 through 2008, with speculation rampant, all real estate was increasing in value daily and appraisers could not keep up with the appreciation. For a time, appraisers were using time adjustments of $1,000 to $2,500 per month for value increases, but in most areas this was too low. In Waianae, on the Island of Oahu, and in Kapoho and Pahoa on the Big Island, that Oprah and The Donald talked about; values doubled and even tripled for most oceanfront properties.

As everyone knows, the bubble popped with the global recession in 2007-2008 and the financial crisis it brought. With the economic downturn came new government regulations and sub-prime lenders became a historical footnote. Real estate values throughout Hawaii and the United States declined, and with the 2,300 pages of the Dodd-Frank Act, mortgages, whether commercial or residential, have become difficult to obtain without first giving up your eldest born and right foot.

It is not to say that Oprah, Donald Trump, or even the Japanese invasion caused the voracious hunger for Hawaiian land because this lust has been around for centuries. What we do know is that real estate is probably one of the most highly desired possessions because it is one of the most tangible assets. Real estate, as an article of trade, is subject to booms and busts, but when all is said and done, it's where great sums of money can be made or lost. People can see it, touch it, feel it, brag about it. For many people in the world, a piece of Hawaii real estate is the greatest possession to have, if they can afford it.

In the real estate world, the carpetbaggers and scalawags have gone for now, but they will be back quicker then jellyfish after a full moon at the first sign of new opportunities. This has always been true, especially in paradise, or as most of the world knows it, Hawaii.

CHAPTER THIRTY-ONE

The Wisdom Of Fools

In 1961, Hawaii became the first state in the nation to enact a condominium law. This new act created an explosion of condominium development through the 1960s to the late 1990s. A condominium is one or more buildings consisting of apartments that are individually owned.

Every condominium is required to have an association of individual owners, and these owners in turn vote for a Board of Directors to manage the property. With this new concept of ownership, property management companies have sprung up everywhere. The management companies are hired by the Boards to administer the fiscal and physical management of the buildings. They also employ, when required, on-site resident managers to oversee them.

You would think this was the most equitable and honorable way to do business and protect the owners. Unfortunately, that has not been the case for some properties because, it appears, with everyone living so close to each other, familiarly does often breed contempt and there are frequently a lot of conflicts in condominiums which spill over to their Boards.

Part of the problem with Boards is, that while most individuals who volunteer are usually good, honest, hardworking and well meaning, there are others who use these Boards as resume' enhancers, for status positioning, for their personal benefit, or simply for love of power to control their neighbors and what goes on at the property. This becomes obvious when Board members, usually the presidents or "Little Napoleons" as I like to call them, strengthen their power and control by refusing to rotate their positions. As a result, incestuous relationships often develop between them, the property management companies and their resident managers.

Over the years I have observed some Board members from various condominium projects intimidate their resident or property managers into doing "favors" for them at no charge, but at a financial cost to the association. This special treatment is often small, like window cleaning, repairs and maintenance of their individual apartment, walking their dog, or even replacing *halekoa* trees with *plumeria* or *ironwoods* because of their personal taste.

From time to time, much larger and costlier situations arise as a result of Board members assuming too much power, like hiring certain painting or roofing companies because they are friends, or, in the worst case scenario, hiring incompetent acquaintances, friends, or relatives of the resident manager for maintenance positions.

As an example, a few years ago a Waikiki condominium that had several military retirees on its Board, hired as its resident manager a recently retired thirty-year Navy veteran who had served on a ship with one of them. The problem was, after so many years at sea under the scrutiny of his superiors, he did not like to be told what to do by anyone, especially women, and the Board president just happened to be a woman.

He also didn't like physical work much, and the only labor most of the residents saw him do was to wash his little black Miata everyday in the loading zone at 7:00 a.m. His greatest activity was roller blading... in the hallways, common areas, and even the parking garage. Maybe it reminded him of his days at sea when he had to roll with the waves.

When he needed to go to the hardware or home improvement store, he roller bladed. Of course, it took half the day and he could never be found on property during work hours, but he sure looked fit and happy. After eighteen months of work piling up and new Board members coming on, he was finally fired, but he didn't go quietly, threatening to shoot Madam President before he vacated his free apartment.

This type of impudence continued when another Board, which was made up mostly of retired teachers and professors, hired one of its own, a former professor of physics, as resident manager. Problem was, he may have been a great teacher and knew the mathematics of matter and energy, but he was at a complete loss when it came to common sense. One day an elderly resident had an "accident" on a late afternoon as residents were beginning to come home from work. There was a trail of poop from the entrance of the parking structure throughout the first level. The manager decided to let the small piles dry and to pick them up in a day or two. Needless to say, the tires from incoming cars spread the feces across three floors and it took a crew of three men two days to scrub it all up and get the smell out.

Even with this stinky circumstance in their faces, one of the retired teachers was heard to say, in defense of his compatriot, "He didn't do anything wrong. I could gut these weasels like fish," when venting his anger toward his fellow Board members who chose to reprimand the manager. While most thought the Board member was just angry, a few other members were intimidated, as he was an ex-Army Ranger from the Vietnam era and had been in special operations for two tours before becoming an instructor. One member resigned shortly after his outburst and two others chose not to run for re-election. The resident manager remained in his job for another three years.

There have even been circumstances when Boards have harassed specific individuals when they, as homeowners, raised complaints over the maintenance and management of their project, as was the case in a lawsuit involving Diamond Head and Kailua condominiums a few years ago. These personal-vendetta driven conflicts have often cost associations hundreds of thousands of dollars in deferred maintenance, legal fees, and judicial judgments when a simple telephone call, personal courtesy, or a meeting would have been enough to resolve the problem.

Sadly, "the wisdom of fools" will continue to rule until more property owners take a larger active role in their associations. It will only be resolved when the "Little Napoleons" are forced off Boards through mandated term limits for Board members, particularly the president. Until then, most condominium homeowners can be assured their maintenance fees will keep going up and special assessments will continue to be levied, and not always because of the consumer price index, inflation, or compelling needs.

CHAPTER THIRTY-TWO

Everyone's An Expert

People often ask me what I believe makes an expert in the field of real estate. I tell them, tongue in cheek, that all business is about personality, style, and sometimes, even knowledge. One of the most interesting observations I've discovered over the years is that so many people believe they are experts in real estate.

People can be florists, carpenters, firemen, musicians, car salesmen, or politicians, but because they, or their best friend, have purchased a property, or maybe they have become strict devotees of HGTV's *Property Virgins* or *House Hunters,* believe they know everything about the real estate business.

There are also the part-time "flippers" who consider themselves authorities. These are people who have never really been in the business but tout themselves as all-knowing because they were lucky enough to have bought, renovated, and resold properties during the go-go years and walked away with $100,000 or more before taxes.

Of course they forget they could have thrown dog poop on the walls for an earthier look, jacked the house up on termite eaten stilts, painted the outside canary yellow, and still doubled their money in those days.

My personal favorites are the ones who explain how they were failures in everything until they found their calling in real estate. These types now have all sorts of self-help books for real estate, DVD's, games, seminars, and infomercials explaining how you too can find wealth and happiness in the business, as long as you buy their products. They often hype themselves as experts in the gold and silver business as well, and include a teaser DVD on the buying and selling of bullion or coins.

Real estate or bullion...I have always found this a fascinating package. My guess is that the bullion is included as a backup for the person who bought their products and can't make it happen in the real estate market. This protects the experts by giving the purchaser an alternative, even though they have been guaranteed success with the $99.99 purchase of their merchandise.

There are also a lot of people in the real estate business who call themselves "full service agents." These people usually provide a rental service for their clients' residential properties. This happens during the down times when things get tough, but again, I believe it would be stretching it to say they are property management experts or experts in general.

Also, I do not consider a newly minted MBA holder with a degree in finance or real estate, who is now a vice president of some large real estate investment trust or fund because his or her relative owns the company, an expert. Of course, they will tell you they are, and insist you do things their way, and their way only.

While I believe architects, engineers, interior designers, and construction managers have certain skills and knowledge of real estate, I don't believe them to be experts either. I've often had to bite my tongue and smile when a middle-aged, unsuccessful architect or construction manager, whose greatest fame was being appointed to a job in the building permit or land use office by some past mayor or governor, and is now in the private sector, has come up and lectured me on his opinions on economic trends and the future of the market.

Also, and I know this will shock many of you, I do not consider someone an expert who is greatly successful in the buying and selling of real estate. This shows me they are good in marketing and selling homes or commercial buildings, but in my opinion, that makes them only great sales people.

Sales, whether cars, insurance, or real estate, are mainly about social networking. When a person is marketing a commodity, they are in effect, selling themselves. If the client is attracted to the salesperson, and the product is right for them, then a deal will be made. Knowledge and understanding of the object of trade often takes a backseat in hot selling markets.

This all became clear to me some years ago when a young ex-Marine, originally from a small town in Iowa, came to Hawaii to get into the insurance business. Strikingly handsome, charming, tall, with light eyes and dark hair, he really stood out. He didn't know a soul on his arrival in Honolulu, but within three weeks, had joined the Honolulu Club, the Elks Club, and the Hawaii Yacht Club, which were affordable over the more pricy Country Clubs, and offered immediate membership and a list of members to prospect for new clients. Everyday of his first year in town he would sit in either his navy blue pinstripe or light gray suit, with a meticulously pressed white shirt, power red tie, and highly polished, black oxfords outside the coffee shop at Bishop Square, the center of Honolulu's financial district. While appearing to read the paper, he greeted everyone who walked by, making eye contact with each person.

He was quick to say he was not the sharpest knife in the box, although I never believed this for a second. He was affable and quick-witted, and if you gave him half a chance, his staff would help you in all your concerns about insurance and annuities.

All of us ladies just adored him; we were only too glad to get our husbands and boyfriends to meet and work with him. When they met him, they too were charmed and introduced their buddies to him as well. Today he's a fixture in the community, very successful, and continually sets and breaks sales records.

Another lure is a real estate agents' business card. Almost all agents have photographs of themselves on their cards to make sure prospective clients remember them. When was the last time you saw an attorney or accountant with his or her face plastered on a card? Agents, because of this need for visual perfection, often use their "make-over" photos with the heavy makeup and hair retouched, or the photo that was taken over twenty years ago on a very good day, and that's just the guys. I don't know about others, but I often have an embarrassing tendency to keep looking at the card and the agent to make sure I am meeting with the same person.

Sales to me are a lot like fishing, much like the days my Dad and I spent on the ocean. You start out by chumming the water through advertising and open houses. Then you get a nibble or two on the line when calls and showings take place. Finally, you get a bite and reel them in for the sale and closing. Luck is often regularly involved and sometimes an unexpected tussle will occur and you lose the fish when the buyer drops out of escrow. However, more often than not, depending on your product, whether it is a high-priced house, a small bungalow, or large acreage, you frequently can hook a couple of big fat marlins or well heeled buyers who are unrepresented by other agents.

So how do I define an expert in the field of real estate?

Experts, I believe, are individuals who have a good, overall understanding of the entire real estate market, from construction, to housing to finance. To be a specialist, they also need a lot of formal education and must never stop learning.

When I first started out in the business, few certifications or designations were available to set one apart from the rest of the pack, and most of these were in the finance or property management end of the business...not marketing. Only interior designers were allowed to stage homes and received substantial fees for this work. In today's world there are certifications and designations for everything from internet marketing to exchange specialists. There are staging experts, lighting experts, color designers, computer specialists, data research experts, solar home experts, certified green specialists, historic home experts, and the list goes on and on.

However, I believe the most important requirement to make someone an expert in real estate is to have at least twenty years of full time experience in the business, covering many different aspects, such as property management, development, and both residential and commercial sales.

Over a span of two decades one can see first hand the different cycles of real estate. These cycles usually occur every six to eight years. Whether or not people are involved in commercial or residential real estate, these ups and downs can be critical for honing their skills, and ultimately give them the knowledge to make them experts in their field.

Or we could just forget this chapter entirely and ask anyone on the street or at the beauty parlor their opinion of the current real estate market, because no matter what I say, everyone will still think of themselves as the ultimate expert. Everyone is an expert...really, just ask 'em!

CHAPTER THIRTY-THREE

Some Deals Are Made In Heaven

One summer morning I was chatting with one of the more successful Honolulu real estate developers about a certain property and complaining about how difficult it was to complete a sales transaction on it. He looked at me for a while and finally said,

"Well, I believe some deals are made in Heaven."

"And many in Hell!" I retorted.

He chuckled, but went on to say, "As you know, deals are a lot like children and often need time to grow, so patience is frequently the answer to everything."

Over the years I have been involved in some fabulous successes and some even more spectacular dooseys. Some deals were so easy they were like catching a wave with only a few strokes, and surfing its crest all the way to shore as the sun was setting over the horizon.

There was a deal back in the 1980s when a young *haole* woman in her mid-twenties from Los Angeles (I later found out her Dad was a famous Hollywood producer), came to my open house, looked around, sat down, and said, "How much?" After I told her the price, she pulled out her checkbook from her Louis Vuitton purse and proceeded to write a $100,000 check for the deposit and down payment. It was a 100% cash purchase and we closed within thirty days.

Or in the early 1990s when I was a listing agent for the owner of a large commercial property and the representative of a newly formed corporation came by and walked around the site. He liked what he saw and pulled out a pre-signed letter from the owner of the company for an offer to lease for half of the building right then and there. The proposal was to pre-pay the rent for the first six months up front, plus a three month security deposit. The transaction was completed in less than ten business days and the now established company is still there today.

However it is very true that the deals which make you a better overall professional are often the ones that have some adversity connected with them. I have been involved in transactions where there were true idiots on both sides, sloppy attorneys, and shady brokers. The coconut wireless of Hawaii is faster than a rocket, and some transactions have been destroyed by gossip and hearsay.

Some dealings have been so problematic that I have often wondered how I ever got caught up in them in the first place. Like when the seller died two weeks before closing and left no beneficiaries for his trust, including his wife of forty years. Or when the interior designer convinced her client to use her massage therapist's husband as the agent instead of me after the initial meeting and even after the offer was drawn up by me because "Helen* gets all my kinks out, she is just so fabulous!" The designer told me I wouldn't understand, and she was right. Or the time the husband and wife were in the middle of a purchase and also getting a divorce, but unfortunately the wife forgot to tell the husband they were splitting and he couldn't understand why the transaction and its documentation were taking so long.

One of my better failures was the sale of Nick's Fishmarket. In September, 1989, Nick's Fishmarket, was the most happening place in Honolulu. It had been going strong for several years and was where the movers and shakers and Hawaii's most beautiful people always hung out.

Another broker and I had a Japanese corporation that wanted to buy the restaurant and expand its concept to Japan. For this privilege they were willing to pay the owners $5,000,000 cash. I was referred by the majority owner of the restaurant, whom I knew, to Randy Schoch, who was a minority owner and operations manager. I had a signed contract and a cashier's check for $500,000 in my hands and was to meet with Randy on Monday morning at 8:00 a.m. sharp.

When I arrived, Randy was not in a good mood. He had just flown in from Los Angeles on the Red Eye after partying all weekend at the Playboy Mansion with his then girlfriend, Miss June of 1989. He was thirty years old, impossibly handsome, six feet one inch tall, extremely fit with the bluest eyes, and full head of blond hair.

The chairs in his office were full of crisply pressed dress shirts and material for trousers and suits. His personal tailor was fluttering about, measuring him for a new wardrobe. He looked at me standing there in my red polo shirt, starched blue jeans, red sneakers and scowled. I found out later he had only been told that some real estate agent was coming to see him and had an offer for the restaurant. He had seen this many times before with no substance behind the bid and he was not amused with me standing there causally dressed and totally unfamiliar to him.

He had a half a dozen expensive watches of all sorts and sizes in a small jewelry box by his telephone and was looking at them. He finally picked the Hamilton watch that looked like it was out of Salvador Dali's painting, *The Persistence of Memory*, and closed the box.

I must have stood there waiting for over fifteen minutes, and all the while he took phone calls and continued to frown at me. My first impression of him was that he might be very handsome and appeared smart, but that he thought way too highly of himself and was a very conceited horse's ass.

Finally he turned his attention to me and said with great disdain, "I know everyone in town who is anybody. I know all the real estate people of importance and I don't know you! Who the fuck are you?"

I looked him straight in the eye and said simply, "I'm the person who has the client who wants to pay you five million dollars cash for your restaurant."

He looked me up and down again for a moment determining if I was telling the truth and then grinned as he said,

"Well, then okay, sit down."

He got up and moved his shirts over to the other chair so I could have a seat.

After our first meeting, we actually grew to like each other and worked well on the deal together. Three weeks before closing, the Japanese got concerned that the entry door to the restaurant faced north, which was bad luck for them.

"Shit, I'll blow a hole in the frickin' concrete and move the entrance to keep them happy," was Randy's response. Problem solved.

In the end, two weeks before closing, the deal died because the owner of the hotel refused to allow the sale and transfer of the restaurant or its name.

I often tell people, if I cried over all the commissions I've lost for whatever reasons I would be thin and dehydrated, but I did have tears when we lost the Nick's deal because we had been so close, and the other broker and I were to receive a full six percent on the sales price as our commission.

Looking back now over the years, however, it all turned out okay in the end. Randy went on to become one of the best restaurant entrepreneurs in the United States, married a wonderful woman, and had two lovely children. The best part is, he and I have remained life-long friends.

What I've learned in real estate is that it's like life in general; it's all about determination and standing up for yourself. Bad situations can either hone you or destroy you. You must believe in yourself and have a strong heart in all you do because you cannot achieve something greater than yourself unless you try something new outside of your comfort zone.

I was truly terrified when I started out in the Real Estate business and then on my own as a consultant, but I wanted a better life without being under someone else's thumb. I was tired of never achieving what I wanted because of that insidious glass ceiling. Perseverance and will power got me through the toughest of times and I learned my failures and successes have always been the result of my own decisions.

As Maya Angelou said, "When you know better, you do better." Know who you are and be true to yourself. Do or do not do; it is ultimately your choice.

As the years have passed, I have learned and my confidence has grown as I have completed each new transaction or report. It feels good to be my own boss, and even though there is still a lot of posturing in the brokerage and consulting business with landlords and other brokers and consultants, there are always opportunities. I still have good years and bad years financially, but like my developer friend said to me, patience is the key. The world is my oyster and I'm still happily looking for the pearl.

And well, it's true that I never did achieve my professional surfing career, I do have sun-bleached hair and I still surf on occasion and hang out with hot surfer dudes although they are now the children of my friends.

So dreams, while not completely as you first imagined, often do come true.

The "Donny and Marie of Hawaii Real Estate" – Steven and me 1977

The Honolulu Merchandise Mart Building Circa 1978

HONOLULU MERCHANDISE
MART

Vol. 1 No. 1   December 1978

From The Manager –
Stephany Sofos

SEASON'S GREETINGS! Well here is the newsletter we have been promising for the past month.

In an attempt to upgrade the Honolulu Merchandise Mart we will be enacting various planned projects throughout the new year, with the emphasis on increased public awareness of the building and the tenants within.

These various projects will include improved janatorial service, planned graphics throughout the building, this newsletter, and promotional activities tentatively scheduled for once a month.

To get our graphics program and newsletter off the ground we invite any and all suggestions in our attempts for we cannot do it all alone. Active participation is the key phrase for the Honolulu Merchandise Mart. For as you know, to keep the warm Hawaiian feeling of the building everyone's help is needed in our attempts.

This participation will start by the volunteering of various talents for the 1st Annual Honolulu Merchandise Mart Christmas Party.

The Christmas Party is scheduled for Thursday, December 21, 1978 from 2:00 p.m. to 6:00 p.m.

We need those talented in entertaining, decorating, eating, etc., to come forward and help.

The Waikiki Lobby of the building is scheduled as the site for the party.

We need Christmas decorations for the walls, a Christmas tree, a Santa Claus (are you reading George Hale?) and anything and everything to make this the best party ever.

So what do you say? Let's get together and do it! Let's have an active participation from one and all to make this a MERRY CHRISTMAS!

If I do not get the chance to see you all at the party, on behalf of Hawaii Management Corporation and myself, I wish you a Mele Kalikimaka e Hauoli Makahiki Hou.

Mart Tenants:

Have a comment about the newsletter or a news item you'd like to see inside? Drop a line to Stephany Sofos, Mart Manager, in Room 446 by the 20th of the month and it will appear in the next edition of the Mart.

Honolulu Merchandise Mart Newsletter

Terry Sousa – 1978

Terry Sousa – 1978

Terry Sousa Today

Hawaii Polo Club Emblem given to me by Jack Madison

Thomas A. Sofos – Midshipmen at Annapolis – 1942

Mom and Dad in 1946

Mom and Dad in 1996 – 50 years later

TASCO's Advertising for their Waialae Nui Ridge Development – 1962

Nalu and Stephany

ABOUT THE AUTHOR

Stephany Sofos was born and raised in Honolulu, Hawaii, and is a graduate of St. Andrew's Priory and the University of Hawaii at Manoa.

She is an active licensed Real Estate Broker and Appraiser.

Stephany has been involved in all aspects of the real estate business for over thirty years and is the only person in the State of Hawaii to earn four international real estate designations concurrently; Certified Shopping Center Manager through the International Council of Shopping Centers, Certified Property Manager through the Institute of Real Estate Management, Real Property Administrator through the Buildings, Owners, Managers Institute, and Graduate of the Realtors Institute of the National Association of Realtors.

Stephany resides in Honolulu with her beloved four legged children.

16035789R00137

Made in the USA
Lexington, KY
30 June 2012